To John +
Hazel

Enjoy the ride

D. W. Le Moine

I Could Have Died
A Thousand Deaths

*Memoirs of a life of adventure,
purpose, and joy on an island in the
San Francisco Bay*

Dave LeMoine

BIG BOOTS
PUBLISHING
REDDING, CA

I Could Have Died A Thousand Deaths

Published in the United States by BIG BOOTS Publishing and CreateSpace, an Amazon.com company. First Edition.

Book cover design by Robert Henslin

ISBN: 1518626319
ISBN-13: 978-1518626319

DEDICATION

To Patty, my best friend and wife of twenty years. Without your encouragement and patience, this book would have never seen the light of day.

I love you, Sabu!

TABLE OF CONTENTS

TABLE OF CONTENTS (Cont.)

<u>Title</u>	<u>Page</u>

TABLE OF CONTENTS (Cont.)

Title   Page

ACKNOWLEDGEMENTS

To my wife, friend, spelling bee champion, author, and editor, Patty. You have the patience of Job!

I am also grateful to the following friends for their encouragement and support:

Jim and Lindy Checchi, for your love and laughter that spurred me on when I didn't think I had it in me.

This would not be nearly as entertaining without my adventurous Shifters friends!

Two hundred firefighter brothers and sisters. Without you, a third of this book could not have been written.

Rob Henslin – Thank you for your expertise and friendship. Your book cover told my entire story in photos.

PROLOGUE

Experience with death came early in my life, through my dad dying in front of me from a little-known genetic factor, Familial Hyper Cholesterol Anemia, or clogged arteries. I was only eight years old at the time and relived his death when I went on my first call in the fire department 19 years later.

I could have died many times in this uncertain world. Here are a few examples:

Young Kid - On Bay Farm Island stuck in shoulder-deep mud.

Teen Years - While crashing cars in the Oakland hills.

At 19 - In a gas explosion at a brass foundry, with molten metal blowing up in my face.

At 29 - In my father-in-law's yacht, which was on fire ten miles off the Southern California coast.

At 48 - Attacked and stoned by Hamas terrorists in Israel, who would have burned us to death.

Thirteen years into my career, the gene that killed my dad was uncovered in me. I thought my life was over, but God had different plans. I now know His hand has been guiding me all this time through:

> The Bay Farm Island Years
> The Happy Days Era
> The Fire Years
> My Spiritual Journey

And now… Here is the rest of my story.

Everything leaves the earth eventually in the physical form, but the memories of good people and good work are timeless!

INTRODUCTION: DAVE'S STORY
What Front Door?
(You Mean That Ball of Flame?)

December 1968, 1:00 a.m.

I was going to my first structure fire, riding the tailboard of a most magnificent red and gold leaf engine, diesel roaring, siren screaming, radio in the background pleading for manpower. Air horn blasting, leaning into a turn with only my two hands clamped on the bar, the one thing keeping me from bouncing on my butt and skidding to a stop, as Engine One's tail lights disappear into the night, was my grip. Me? I'm a nervous new kid semi-secure in the knowledge that I'm standing next to Moe Hale. Moe is extremely confident and anxious to get into the battle. As I look ahead, with a mix of apprehension and excitement, I see a fully involved two-story apartment, with Pete silhouetted in the flames.

Moe yells, "The captain will have us go through the front door."

I ask in a somewhat agitated voice, *"What front door? You mean that ball of flame?"*

The reply comes, "Yeah, no sweat." I think to myself, *Who, me? Nah.* But then I see Moe's brother, Bob, crawling out of the building. His Scott Air Pack valve had just broken off in a fall down the stairs and was discharging 2500 pounds of pressure from the cylinder.

With great concern, Moe rolls his brother over and asks, "Bobby are you okay?"

With steam rising from his turnout coat and a smile on his face, Bob replies weakly, "Yeah, I'm okay."

Moe grabs him by the coat, leans close in and threatens, "Just you wait until I tell mom!"

I know then that I am in the company of men of uncommon valor. *I love this job!*

Back to reality, we're through the front door and beating back the flames. *This isn't so bad, when you have a team around you.* As the fire dies into darkness, my eyes haven't adjusted yet from bright as day to midnight black. My Maglight's beam doesn't penetrate the dark, dense smoke. It seems more like a penlight than the floodlight we need in here. I'm on all fours crawling, groping, throwing things out of the way, feeling for people (hoping not to find any), into closets, under beds, behind doors. *Where are they? Maybe they're already out.*

Then, as if a light switch has been turned on, the room clears of smoke. Is it a miracle? No, the truck crew must be on the roof chopping holes. *Now that's fun!* I think my favorite thing in life is to be sitting astride the ridge of a three-story Victorian at 2:00 a.m., axe in hand, smoke rising from the great hole we just opened, the floodlight almost blinding as I gaze down from my perch to the street below, the aerial ladder nearby. It's the only means of escape if the roof starts to collapse. Firefighters look like ants running and pulling hoses in all directions. Muffled yells come from inside the house as they find and are attacking the fire. *No better place to be. This job has given me a real purpose in life, and I even get paid for it. Thanks, God.*

The fun is over with 2,000 feet of wet, dirty hose to roll and pick up. The adrenalin is gone. I'm soaked from head to toe, but our spirits are high. Again, training and teamwork take control. The mood is light; tension from the sometimes-long wait between fires has been relieved. Back at the station, everyone joins in to reload Engine One with dry hose. The truck's equipment is cleaned and returned to its rightful cabinets.

"Hey Cap, we can go back in service!"

A warm shower followed by dry clothes feel great. I'm so relaxed. Daylight is breaking in the east. I could go back to bed, but... *is that the smell of bacon and coffee?* Most of the guys are in the kitchen talking and laughing about old George, Crash, and Harry, or the gracefulness of me tripping over a 2-1/2 inch hose in the middle of the street.

Pete says, "We thought you were a klutz, but now we're positive."

My reply: "Oh yeah, I'm sure most of you have been on your face a time or two!"

"Attention all stations!" *Uh oh! Here we go again.*

I guess I'll finally get some sleep at home today.

3

I Could Have Died A Thousand Deaths

As we approach the address, in the headlights of our fire rig, we see a man holding a Cabbage Patch Doll. No! It's a baby.

A Gift that Keeps on Living
(She Feels Like My Daughter In My Arms)

Station Four, Winter of 1983

I'm a lieutenant at Alameda Fire Station Four. John is the engineer with firefighter Mike; we are looking forward to a quiet shift. Bay Farm Island is in the suburbs. The Island, as it was called, is actually a peninsula connected to Oakland with only one way in and out, across a bridge that connects Bay Farm to Alameda proper. The island had been expanded by fill to three times its original size. Therefore, we had to move a double-wide trailer up next to the drill tower until a new station could be built.

The only thing that keeps us awake that afternoon is the constant thud of golf clubs on the second hole and an occasional ball bouncing off my office wall. A trip to the store, some familiarization, and back home for a quick workout, and the day will be done. The workout room is situated on the fourth floor of the tower, probably the tallest building in the east end. A six foot square poster of my brother Jim in a Raiders uniform is on the back wall, with a few dead flies swept aside that need to be vacuumed, and me astride the exercise bike with the smell of sweat, smoke, and dry rot in my nostrils.

4

Looking down from my perch, I see before me a concrete wall that divides Island Drive from the golf course. The wall extends one-

half mile to a bridge. Across the bridge, in the setting sun with street lights coming on, sits the city of Alameda. *Sure glad I'm on the quiet side tonight.* As the light dims, my eyes focus again on the wall, now in the moonlight.

I walked that wall as a boy at least once a week, just to see if I could. I sat on that wall at seven years old to watch fire-fighters training, engines revving, ladders extend-

ing, men running, and water spraying. That wall carried me home in the dark after football practice, with no school bus that time of night. That wall saw Dad's first heart attack while lifting heavy hose in training evolutions. That wall exhibits the scars from our '51 Chevy bumper, sparks lighting the night. That wall is still there 37 years later separating me from a now four-lane divided boulevard. That wall says to me, "Come on down, Dave. I'm still here. You want to try me again? I won't move." The other side of that wall is Island Drive, flowing up and over the bridge into the city I call my home.

As Mom tells it, I was about one year old when we left Los Angles for Oakland, from there to 1721 Schiller Street, Alameda. Dad joined the Alameda Fire Department in 1942. Brother Jim came along three years later. One of my earliest recollections was of Mom in a long coat in the night being taken to the hospital to give birth to my brother. Biff Hoffman, an off-duty firefighter friend, was there to help as Dad was on duty. The fire department had truly become our extended family. My paternal grandmother lived with us, a neat old lady with white hair and very proper manner. Her husband, my grandad, had died. Grandad retired from Richmond Fire in 1917, as chief of the department. My uncle had been the mechanic for Richmond in the days of horse-drawn steamers and later retired as an engineer.

The day of Jim's homecoming was exciting. I can remember Mom being in bed, Grandma changing Jim and getting squirted. He grew from 8 to 260 pounds and played football for Alameda High, the Buffalo Bills, Houston Oilers, and Oakland Raiders, then much later died in the line of duty working for Alameda County Fire. Now his son, Jason, has followed his dad into the fire service to become the LeMoine's fifth generation of firefighters. Dad worked at Station Three at Grand and Pacific, which was about three blocks from home. At age four, playing on the sidewalk in front of the house, I would often hear Engine Three's sirens, and ride my tricycle to Buena Vista Avenue, to wave at Dad and his friends as they raced by. That began my love and understanding of the fire department. Dad would take me into the station where the aroma of smoke from their turnouts, gasoline from the rigs, and food cooking was quit a mix. It wasn't until 1968, ten years in the trades and six of those at Peterson Caterpillar Tractor, that I decided to try for the fire department. On re-entering Station Three to visit my step-father-in-law, Warren (Red) French, the odor was the same, taking me back to my childhood with Dad's strong hand holding mine. I knew where I belonged. It was my destiny.

Returning to reality, it's 6:00 p.m., dinner is over, the television is on in the dayroom. Life is good. As I finish my reports, it is shaping up to be a quiet night. Eight p.m., in bed, watching television, and thinking *I'll sleep through the night.*

Nine p.m., tone alert, **"Attention all stations, we have a still** (response) **for Engine Four to the 300 block of Maitland Drive, the report of a three month old child not breathing."**

The heartrending words that move even the slowest firefighter. In one motion I am in my turnouts, down the hall, and onto the engine. We clear the apparatus room door, left on Mecartney, left on Maitland. I know these streets like the back of my hand; in fact, I know almost everyone in every house we pass. *There's the corner store where I was almost run over by my friend, and the apartment that belonged to Sharon, my second girlfriend.*

"It's about three blocks down, John," I yell. No real need to say anything to John; he knows his job. Somehow the talking calms me.

"One more block," I shout. Approaching the cross street, I look to my left and see Mom's house in the distance.

As we pass Melrose Avenue, I see in the headlights a man coming out from between two parked cars carrying what looks like a Cabbage Patch doll. John pulls to a stop as I clear the cab and move into the headlights. I reach for his daughter and can see that she is blue. He starts to hand her to me but pulls back reluctantly; I reassure him and he releases his grip. She is so small, maybe eight pounds, too small for the breathing equipment on our rig. I think to myself, *Rescue One is two minutes out. She feels like my daughter in my arms.* Against protocol, I start mouth-to-mouth by sucking. I

7

can feel a good air exchange, and then I give her light puffs. Her color returns; she has a pulse. I feel such an urgency to get her to the hospital; I turn and start to move alongside Engine Four in the direction of the ambulance, as if it would make any difference. But a few feet is a few feet closer to the Paramedics, which is a few feet closer to the hospital. By then, I could see Medical One two blocks away. I still have a good air exchange but no response. The ambulance is on the scene. It is great to see Mike, the only Paramedic in Alameda Fire at the time.

"Mike, I got a clear airway. Her color is returning but she's not responding."

The three of us get in the back of the ambulance and the driver takes off for Emergency. Protocol, again, calls for strapping the patient down. One belt across her stomach; it is bordering on the ridiculous. Mike has her on O/2. I try flicking her foot with no response, *Come on, kid. Breathe!* Emergency has been alerted; we are moving fast. Again, past that familiar concrete wall, over the bridge, down Otis, right on Willow, then into the hospital parking lot. As we pull up to the door, we see four nurses and two orderlies. A little overkill except, after all, it's a baby.

No need for the gurney. Mike carries her into the operating room and onto the bed, she is still non-responsive. Five more minutes, which seem like hours, and my job is done as I back against the wall to make room for the pros. She takes a long, urgent breath and starts kicking and crying. I look around the room to see that everyone is in tears.

Returning to Station Four, we again pass by my wall back into the apparatus room, and try to settle our hearts which are still pumping too much adrenalin. As we chat quietly at the table, no one seems to want to leave the fellowship of this band of brothers for bed. Satisfaction settles in and soon we know that we were here this day for the real **purpose-driven life**. What started as a slow day ended in adrenalin, elation, and exhaustion. That's what we do... just another day in paradise.

At home the next day I share the story with my two daughters.

They agree that the baby and her sister need stuffed animals for Christmas. A quick visit and all is well in the world, for now. It turns out that the little girl is a twin and both girls had a fixable esophageal birth defect. A trip to Children's Hospital in Oakland, an operation on both, and they are okay.

Eight years future, while running the engine at a fully involved house fire, with the fire out, and things settling down, our job became returning equipment to the rig. We call it "mopping up." I am approached by an unfamiliar woman with a tap on my shoulder. As I turn, she says with a warm smile, "Dave, you don't know me but I know you. You saved my baby. She's now in third grade. She and her sister are doing great. Thank you!"

As she walks away into history, I am left standing there without words. We don't always have successful saves, but victories like this are enough to pay for the bad calls that are inevitable. Community service with God's help, that's what firefighters do. I am truly blessed.

9

I Could Have Died A Thousand Deaths

What, then, makes me who I am? First - a great mother and father who struggled to plant us in a safe place called Bay Farm Island, a poorer suburb of Alameda. Second - surrounded by a larger fire family, sometimes referred to as the AFD. Third - born to be the fourth generation of that fire family going back to the 1880's, which shaped my brother and me and set our life paths. Fourth - born in the greatest time in history. Here, now is a 53 year snippet of my ongoing life. I am still in process, but not finished with, the rest of my story.

So, let's start from the beginning...

PART ONE

Alameda, My Home Town
(The Growing Up Years)

This is the way it was in the 40s, 50's and 60's in a great American city called Alameda, in a much simpler time. Where money was tight, people worked hard, and a friend could be greeted on Park Street for coffee. A time when Tucker's ice cream cones were less than a buck, Ole's served up amazing waffles, and the smell of chicken frying as you passed by Lola's restaurant could bring you to your knees; Lincoln and Franklin Park's picnics on Sunday afternoons; cruising South Shore in my '32 Ford. And the biggest traffic bottleneck, once a year, was at High Street and Thompson Avenue (Christmas Tree Lane), Santa in the center divider, with people passing and children laughing in a holiday mood. We would periodically become stuck in traffic, waiting for the bridge to close after the Johnny Peterson tugboat, with barge in tow, passed through for Tidewater Sand and Gravel. The Fourth of July parade, driving Fire Engine One. Firemen sitting in front of old Station One on Webb Avenue, leaning back on the antique captain's chairs talking with the kids, and families together in a city called Alameda, attached to a landmass called Bay Farm Island.

I Could Have Died A Thousand Deaths

Memories of Bay Farm Island

I am now retired from the Alameda Fire Department, living in Redding, California, but always return to my home, Bay Farm Island. As a child of eight, arriving home in our driveway at night, we could see forty pairs of eyes staring back at us in the headlights, those crazy jack rabbits! They used to run through the airport by the thousands in the 40's and 50's, stopping takeoffs and landings, until men with shotguns and my dog Bark culled the herds. I can remember delivering many *Times-Star* and *Tribune Newspapers* to the whole island as well as a few farmhouses. I hated the winter nights with that bay headwind blowing, long dirt road bike trips for four or five farms. But now the memories are great. The perspective of the farmers is one look at Bay Farm. But the 15 to 20 kids who migrated in, and combed every square inch of our Island, saw this land with a different set of eyes.

Here's more of the story: I was born in 1941. My family moved to Bay Farm Island in 1947, the second Alameda Fire family to arrive; Frank Lufkin and his family preceded us, living on Garden

Dad and Brother Jim 1947

Road. The Beach Road group of firemen came next. My dad and mom bought the lot at 255 Beach Road and, with the help of Dad's firefighting buddies, cleared a plot of land next to Godfrey Park.

Dad built a small, 800 square-foot dwelling and, after he died in 1949, Russ, Ben and some of the other fire guys added two bedrooms, a bath, and garage to make things easier for us. Our

12

family was the first of 12 fire families to build on Beach Road, followed by Red French, Tex Evans, Jimmy Smith, Brad Nichols, Ben Eardahl, and Russ Smith. Then came Bob DeCelle; Bill Simon, across from the park; and further down, Archie Waterbury; Noel Van Derhagen; and Clark Magby. As I write today, September 21, 2015, I am viewing the video of a house fire. In the video are Engine Four, Engine One, and Truck One pulling up to extinguish a fire at 219 Beach Road. Ironically, the house was built by Jimmy Smith (an Alameda fireman), my dad, and a dozen or so firefighters around 1949 or '50 with me looking on. Sixty-five years later, I am witnessing its destruction and am the only one that can tell this story.

Most of those small houses were partially built with scrounged lumber removed from military barracks torn down after World War II. As a 7 year old, I spent my free time at the Godfrey Park sandbox, or watching the firemen help each other in home construction. I later followed my dad into that fire family, and had a great 25-year career serving our city. The chief who hired me was Ernie Servente. I can still remember him crawling out from under our house, as his part in our construction was the plumbing.

Beach Road was gravel then. The only paved road on all of Bay Farm Island was Maitland Drive. In those years, if you had any reason to go to the Main Island, you would cross a two-lane, center-pivot bridge that, in the winter, could be closed a couple of times a year for a super-high tide. Dropping off the bridge onto a two-lane road, you would see to your right a 15 foot-high gravel dike that extended all the way to open farmland. The dike held back the bay water. The other side of this dike was the future location of Harbor Bay Isle.

Dike

The dike was located in what is now the center divider of Island Drive. The other side had that infamous concrete wall separating Island Drive from the Alameda Golf Course. The year of 1947 also brought our Alameda Fire Department drill tower, the tallest structure on the east end of town. It's still standing, though condemned, at the entrance of Alameda Golf Course.

That wall still brings back such memories! At 17, after football practice, with no school bus to ride at that time of the night, I would walk from Thompson Field, down Park Street, and run to High Street *(uphill both ways),* over the bridge to the wall, climb and walk, or run, the wall past the tower, or I would walk the top of the dike looking across the mudflats and see the destroyers in the distance silhouetted in the setting sun. Much of the time, I could travel from the bridge to Maitland Drive without seeing a car.

During the Korean War, there was a military artillery base and radar emplacement with bunkers at the corner of Maitland and Island Drive. Continuing on down Island, it ended in farm fields, now Mecartney Road. Making a right turn onto a dirt road, along the mudflats, this area is now part of Harbor Bay. Further down the dirt road stood a couple of old houses on pilings; the houses would have water under them at high tide. The owner of one of the houses, I believe his name was Lehi Torrey, had accumulated old buoys, floats, and all kinds of water vehicles, from balsawood rafts to landing barges. Past the houses, through a cable gate onto the Ratto farm and out to the end of the road was a great sandbar, turning left to eucalyptus trees and a duck blind on stilts over the water. Continuing left around the point, following the waterfront, you would pass a wonderful beach house with plate glass windows, a patio and, what looked to me like, Hawaiian outrigger canoes on either side.

Returning to this wonderful beach, you would turn right to a row

World War I , Destroyers under Aughinbaugh

of World War I ships that had been sunk as a dike to protect the area between that point and Island Drive. The dike had failed sometime in the 1930's, and the land had been reclaimed by the fish and ducks. Seemingly, only the farmers and Islanders, as we called ourselves, knew about and used this beach.

Nearing High Tide

The farmers treated us well, allowing us to roam freely on their property. What fun! We called the ships "destroyers," climbing and exploring all over them. The ships had rusted through in many places and were very treacherous for the uninitiated. If you looked down through the rusted decks into the ship's holds, you would see sharks, stingrays, and striped bass swimming in and out, a boy's paradise. Leaving that beach, we would travel the gravel road all the way to Melrose and Maitland Drive. Down Melrose, you would cross Beach Road and go directly into our driveway. Standing in the driveway, to the left was Godfrey Park, straight ahead you had a clear, unobstructed view all the way to the Olivera and Silva farms at Maitland and Fitchburg. Again, down a dirt road toward the end of what is now Oleander and Magnolia, stood the Silva/Soares and Olivera private beach. Only we Islanders were granted access.

Summers would find us at the private beach, which lay in a natural notch that collected mountains of driftwood from all over the bay. Many mounds of timbers, logs, piling, planks, balsawood, and Navy rafts no longer needed (probably from World War II), had been discarded or fallen off ships. They made great paddleboards and floats for swimming. We built rooms on the beach large enough to stand in, then covered them with the driftwood. No one passing by had any inkling there were secret rooms inside; to them it was just a giant pile of driftwood. Behind Beach Road lay open fields all the way to the old Oakland Airport, more military bunkers, and a shooting range full of broken clay pigeons.

Between our house and the course lay fields of grass. Bill, Steve, Jerry, Harvey, Mickey, Tom H., Tom C., Kenny, Norman, the McGregor brothers, Jim, and I built flat-bottom swamp boats one summer to explore the cattail-clogged waters of our kingdom. We caught mallard ducks and jack rabbits. At that time, the Beach Road gang would challenge the Garden Road gang to rock wars. Armed with the finest round rocks, pockets bulging to the point of pants cuffs dragging, with garbage can lids held high, we would attack in a hail of stones and a few tears. That is, until one or more of the moms would shout from their porches, "Enough already! You'll shoot your eyes out!"

To the west was the 18-hole golf course. Between our house and the course lay these fields of grass, two cattail-encircled ponds (now part of the newer 18-hole course), with a strange anomaly I

The Cracks

BARK

couldn't explain, giant fissures in the ground. We called them the "cracks." Snaking all over the open areas, these cracks, some as deep as three feet, and three to four feet wide, were perfect to build forts. Scattered in the four foot high grass around the cracks were great two-foot diameter balls of sunbaked clay. We would stack these balls in circles two high, then cover the top with plywood. The forts would seem to disappear in the tall grass and were perfect for planning night sorties to the golf course while smoking rolled up brown paper bags. We learned quickly not to suck too hard or you could taste a little flame with the smoke. After dark, faces blackened and on a low crawl, we could retrieve a bucket of balls from the shallows of the course ponds in a half hour. There was money to be made but always cognizant of the night patrolling grounds keeper, Ed Arata, who scared us to death. The golf balls could then be sold to a neighbor who cleaned and resold them to the course, kind of like early recycling. Through responses to my stories, I finally understand that the cracks were caused by liquefaction during earthquakes sometime in the ancient past, but still no answer about the balls.

Over the years, we dug connector channels, tying crack to crack, so that we could move without being seen from the surface over many acres. At intervals, we would cover a part of a crack with plywood, backfill with dirt and, "Voila!" an underground room. With .22-caliber rifles slung over our shoulders, we roamed these fields, beaches, and farms stopping our conversations just long enough to watch DC-3's or TWA Constellations (nicknamed Connies) coming in for a landing. An added treat would be an occasional B-36 or flying wing passing over. No kid could have had a better environment growing up. In bed at night, as the planes descended over our bedroom for a landing, you could see the flames from the exhaust, a true sound and light show.

We were seen as the poor kids, a little different, the other side of the dumps, in the farms. It was our secret, and very few of the Mainlanders, as we called the kids on the main island, knew of our paradise that lay just over the bridge. A hermit lived behind the dumps near the Oakland border close to the Raiders training facility. We would spend a great deal of time sneaking up on him, telling stories about how much he loved to eat children. If the truth were known, he just wanted to be left alone.

One summer (the year escapes me) arriving at the private beach, we saw a great dredge anchored maybe 200 yards out in the bay. As summer progressed, an island appeared and, off of this island, the water was deep enough to dive from the edge of the sand; there had never been deep water here before. We would swim out every afternoon after the dredge quit and jog the island, which could be a little treacherous due to liquefaction. Running along, you could sink to your chests, and have to breaststroke to get out... not too smart, but we lived.

After one of these long days of sinking in the mud, covered with that bay residue, I arrived home.

Mom said, "You're not coming in <u>my</u> house looking like that! Hose yourself off, remove your clothes in the garage, and then you can enter."

As I pulled off my wet, almost new, T-shirt, it tore apart in my hands. Thinking back now, we had been dipping in all sorts of chemical-laced sand from the bottom of the San Francisco Bay which had accumulated over the centuries, and didn't have a clue of the danger. There were probably heavy metals, and maybe a nuke or two. That might be why I am bald today! A note to the

Low Tide

residents of Harbor Bay Isle if you're having trouble growing plants: Remember that you are sitting on sand sucked from the bottom of the bay near Yerba Buena Island.

I Could Have Died A Thousand Deaths

As time passed, that small island continued to grow and soon became a dike that extended from the end of Maitland around to the San Leandro Marina. As the dike was completed, a set of pipes

Dike Surrounding the Oakland Airport Before it was Filled in

was installed through it near Maitland, to allow the water level inside the dike to maintain bay level. That meant that, on an outgoing tide, you had to keep your distance for fear of being sucked through the pipe to the bay side. On the incoming tide, great four-foot torrents of water would explode from the pipes. We could stand above the superstructure of these pipes, dive into the waterfall, and be projected along the sandy bottom as far as we could hold our breath, then sometimes feeling

the sand sharks and bass spookily rubbing up against us.

At this time, we hadn't a clue that we were swimming in what would become the new Oakland Airport. When the dike was finished, it was time to fill in the airport. The pipes were sealed at low tide and evaporation took over. As the water dried up, the fish inside were trapped. Soon water was reduced to small ponds teeming with fish. People would congregate around these ponds to take home their limits. Eventually, we could reach down and grab the fish by the tail; the hardest part was transporting them home for dinner.

In the sand, which had once been covered by bay water, appeared the wreckage of aircraft that had crashed over the life of the old Oakland Airport. The skeletons of a couple of rusted World War II fighters, with guns still attached, were found… just another benefit for the Bay Farm Island boys.

Soon another dredge and fill project – Harbor Bay Isle – changed the face of Bay Farm Island forever. No more farms, no more destroyers, no more duck blinds, a new bridge, no more cracks, no more dumps or sloughs, no more private beaches. Open acres became tightly packed, two-story houses, as progress came to my wonderful little island.

In earlier days, we could walk from Maitland along the water's edge, all the way around our island to the bridge in about three hours. While beachcombing, shooting our .22's at bottles and debris, or passing an occasional duck hunter, we talked and dreamed of our futures. This is just a snippet of my memories as a boy in paradise. The island – the Ratto, Silva, Sores, and Olivera farms, the close-knit families, and no locks or keys for our homes – was truly a sanctuary for a boy who had lost his dad at age 8, but was safe and secure in this simple spit of land called Bay Farm Island.

Part Two

Dave Meets Dean ("Happy Days" Prototype)
(A Few Years in the Life of Some Local Teens)

Shifters Car Club, Circa 1958

Remembering our "Happy Days" experience of 56 years ago, I'm thinking of a warm summer afternoon. This 17 year old sits on the curb right in front of Jill Jabor's corner store, at Maitland and Flower Lane pondering life.

The roar of a Chevy pickup shatters the quiet and slams me back to reality as it slides to a stop. *Who's the nut trying to kill me?* Out jumps a skinny kid talking to me.

Later Jill Jabor's Store

"Hi, I'm Dean!" he says. "I just hotwired my dad's truck and am going for a cruise. Ya wanna go?"

"Yeah!" I reply.

I was in the seat of this now-vintage pickup (*I can still smell the interior*). And off we went. I felt free as we drove up High Street to the Oakland Hills. Dean was full of mischief, burning rubber around corners, chasing cats, jumping curbs, and driving through a row of thoughtfully planted flowers. What fun *(though I don't condone the mischief)*! Friendship, common goals, cars, and dreams, that's what we were all about.

Dean got away with being the family car thief for quite a while. The first time I heard the Johnny Cash song, "Ring of Fire," was in Dean's front room. At the time we hadn't a clue that we were beginning what's become 57 years of friendship.

Bay Farm Island 1957 - Beyond the Dumps

My love of cars and trucks had probably started with the smell of Station Three at age 3. By age 15, in 1956, mom would often let me drive the Olds the last couple of blocks home without a permit. We lived next to Godfrey Park. Marion, the Park Director, owned a red and white 1954 Buick Roadmaster hardtop. She would let me drive her car the half-block to my house for a wash job. What a deal! Her son had a 1950 Chevrolet fastback with a louvered hood, loud pipes and a left-handed column shift, quite unique. Some days she would drive the Chevy to work. Well, it was my first chance to drive a stick. What fun, grinding, jerking and gunning the engine.

In the summer of 1958 I worked for a landscaping business where I learned to drive their ten-wheel dump truck on my permit, and we actually got away with it! By age 22 I had owned 17 cars, assorted Model A's, and a wreck of a '32 Ford roadster that became my show and street machine. Three of those cars were for destruction derbies. They were bought for $110 from a used car lot. I should have put them in the garage instead of demolition, as they would be worth more like $50,000 today.

Genesis of the Shifters

Dean and I had met Benton Randolph III, known as Red Dog for his flaming red hair, in auto shop. Soon we were introduced to his brother, Frank; Lee, who went by the nickname Budda; and Phil, called Flip. Flip lived above the corner store at Encinal Avenue and High Street with his father and brother.

Then there was Ken, or Heater (at more formal events, Heaterbill). Afterward came Gary; John; Laurence, later the owner of "The Acapulco," a great Mexican restaurant; and Jerry who was a neighbor from BFI. Frank named me Uncle Boobs for my barrel chest. Thanks, Frank!

After completing my '32 Ford, powered by a supercharged '55 Olds engine, with 24 coats of pearlescent blue paint and candy apple red racing stripes, my name became Lead Foot. Corvettes? No problem.

We started meeting at the Randolph's home and then moved to our clubhouse in Laurence's mom's basement on Buena Vista Avenue.

First Car

It took me all summer working for a landscaper to save $300 for a '49 Chevy. I added a louvered and primed hood, some gold moon hubcaps, and a P.A. system in the grill so everyone could hear "Wake up Little Suzy" as we passed by. It had a left-handed column shift for faster second gear, and new seat covers.

49 Chevy

In the meantime, Mom had just bought a red '56 Ford station wagon from a cattle ranch. We didn't have the money to remove the "Action Ranch" sign, so we erroneously became the proud owners of a ranch.

Mom never knew what fame the "Action Ranch" drew all over Alameda. The cops knew it, the kids at Encinal High School (our rivals) knew it, and Ryders Drive-In parking lot knew it. We used to take a set of coil springs secured from our auto wrecker, jack up the rear end, and fit them between the leaf springs. Instant super rake! Man, I could burn rubber around corners, and destroy tires fast at Mom's expense. Mom kept commenting about the poor grade of tires. *Sorry Mom.*

Dean had a maroon '49 Mercury; Red Dog had a black '50 Ford. He had a real talent for speed shifting second gear; his talent often extended to the destruction of that second gear, and he soon became a pro at changing the Ford transmissions, in about 30 minutes from start to finish. He kept the wreckers rebuilding boxes for $12.50 a pop.

Happy Days and the Fonz

Our first encounter with Fred *"the Fonz"* Gaspar, took place kitty corner from Alameda High School at Ryders Drive-In, which was at Oak Street and Central Avenue. Fred was 10 years older, drove a '48 Ford pickup, and had a reputation that scared us to death. He was a fighter and a motorcycle racer, the epitome of COOL. Truly, we were the "Happy Days" prototype 17 years before the television show aired. (I was a jock, but more the Richie character.)

Well, Freddy adopted our group, and we moved as a team... Fremont Drag Strip, Pacheco Speedway, hardtop racing on Saturday nights, girlfriends in tow, proudly wearing our Shifters jackets, and smoking Havana-Tampa cigars. Steaming the windows at Island Drive-In, and constantly working on our cars at the Randolph's, or Budda's on Harvard Drive, or my driveway on Beach Road, blackened from oil and grease. *Poor Mom.* Ken had an Oldsmobile powered '47 Plymouth coupe. We couldn't afford a chain hoist to install the engine, so just brute force was applied. Straddling the engine, feet on the frame, with the chain over my shoulders, I lifted a big block engine enough to bolt up the motor mounts. My body reminds me every morning of this stupidity.

Red and Frank had the coolest home positioned on the estuary, a deep-water channel separating Alameda from Oakland. The Randolph home at 3019 Marina Drive was small, maybe 900 square feet. All the fun was in the backyard. A path on the right side of the house led us through a grape arbor gate to a small yard, with a fish pond to the right, and concrete steps descending to the lower level across the seawall and onto a 65 foot pier. Moving onto the pier was a workshop with a 600 square-foot building, complete

Oakland Alameda Estuary

with family room, bath, kitchen, and a fireplace.

To the right of the building was an open deck; below was a small sand beach which was exposed only at low tide. Further out, near the deep-water end of the deck, sat a covered boat lift concealing a beautiful, 1932 Chris Craft-type inboard ski boat named the Chiquita. Standing at the end of the pier below was a 30-foot-wide, wood and Styrofoam float, a perfect takeoff point for waterskiing.

Industrial buildings and a scrap iron yard were visible across the estuary. Tidewater Sand and Gravel tugboats and barges passed by daily, sounding the horn for the High Street Bridge to open. I could hear that horn wherever I was in town.

At this time, we had very little money and were always looking for any form of income to pay the 20 cents per gallon fee for cruising the Plaza or Gordon Drive-Ins on Friday and Saturday nights. We

sometimes sat for six hours nursing a cherry Coke and an order of French fries. Part-time work at the Chevron gas station at the corner of High and Fernside helped some, and it was a great place to work on our own cars.

One of our sources of income was located across the estuary in the Randolph's rowboat at night. This was done during low tide, stealthily crawling along under the pier looking for brass and copper that had fallen onto the beach during barge loading. These finds would then be sold across town to a scrap iron yard that later resold back to the estuary yard - *maybe the first true recycling plan.*

This lasted until that fateful night under the pier on a 12 inch-wide walkway, face to face with four yellow eyes and two glistening sets of fangs. Guard dogs had been employed.

I Could Have Died A Thousand Deaths

Hmm, Dobermans or water? We boys went for a swim and began looking for other forms of income... like a syphon hose.

Dave and Jerry

Jerry Green was like a brother. I spent a lot of time at his house on Garden Road, which was just next door to Dan and doors, looking across the street, were farmlands all the way to the bay. Jerry's dad, Dave, was an Alameda fireman - a kind, wonderful man, and another father figure. I had the privilege of working for him during his last year as an assistant chief in the Alameda Fire Department.

Mrs. Green adopted me. I loved to sit in her kitchen, eat, and listen to the banter and an occasional strong word or two with friends and family; there was always someone in that kitchen. Jerry's uncle and aunt would arrive on their Harleys or in their cool '41 Ford, two-door sedan, equipped with glass pack mufflers, louvered hood and three carbs. Man, did I love that car!

Flaming Studebaker

Jerry's dad drove an old, brown Studebaker truck that was left in their garage when Dave was at work. Jerry and I had been thinking that the old truck needed a little upgrading. So, with pencils in hand, we sketched flames all over the hood and front fenders. To us, they looked so good, we thought they needed to be permanent. Having found a can of red house paint and a three inch brush, we completed our creation. *What could it hurt?*

I wasn't at the garage when Dave saw his truck, but Jerry did live to grow old, and the truck was driven around with flames. So, just maybe, he liked it. I need to ask Jerry.

28

Shifter-ettes

As time went on, we paired off with girlfriends: Jerry with Judy; Dean with Joanne; me with Sharon and then Shari, Laurence and Donna; Red, Frank, Heater, and Budda with assorted girls. Fred had been adopted into the Canepa family and would take the twin girls, Diane and Doris, everywhere. He became their big brother, and then came his lifelong companion, Bev. Later on, Diane and Doris became cheerleaders. Diane paired with my brother, Jim, and in their senior year, Jim broke a list of football records as tight end. Cheered on by the twins at Thompson Field with their pompoms waving, we beat Berkeley 47-7 for the championship.

Jim and Diane soon married, went off to Utah State University with a full ride scholarship, and then onto pro football, and finally, to Alameda County Fire Department and a busy life together. Unfortunately, they both died before their time.

Paradise on the Estuary

Ben and Joanie Randolph lived on Marina Drive, 17 houses from the High Street Bridge. They loved having us teens around; it also gave them control, we knew that Ben was in charge, and we loved being there. *Another father figure*. Adopted, fed, loved, and disciplined, it was the place to be on the weekends.

Chiquita

We loved to help Ben set and repair pilings located under the pier. Weekends would find the gang on skis behind the Chiquita, sometimes three abreast.

29

I Could Have Died A Thousand Deaths

Navigating from their home, we flew down the channel, waving to the neighbors as we passed, then out into the San Leandro Bay, followed by a 180 degree turn, hoping we didn't fall and hit bottom which was pudding-type mud. After the turnaround at high speed, we made a return trip past the house, through the Fruitvale Bridge, another 180 and back to their pier.

As we passed the house, we could see 20 kids standing on the pier throwing water balloons. They had a homemade diving board at the end of the pier and, depending upon the level of the tide, you could dive maybe 12 feet to the water if you had the nerve.

The Raft

Mom worked for Trans Ocean Airlines and was given an obsolete, twenty-man life raft. What fun. "Let's use it to float the estuary!" How can we inflate this giant blob of rubber without the C02 bottles? We decided to just blow it up by mouth.

Stretched out on the Randolph's front lawn, which covered most of

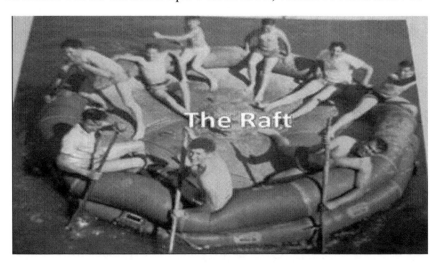

their yard, ten guys began blowing at every inflation point until blue in the face, some totally covered by the raft, and some with only feet showing. Two hours later, it was floatable. But now what?

Twelve feet in diameter and about two feet high, it wouldn't fit through the side gate to the water. So the ten of us with twenty legs, supporting a giant yellow donut, lifted it overhead to clear the tops of cars, moved it down Marina Drive a quarter mile, across the Fruitvale Bridge, which stopped traffic in both directions, and launched upstream of the house.

We drifted on the incoming tide through the old, center-pivot bridge, past the floats, boats, and neighbors waving from their houses, where Ben retrieved us with the Chiquita. When not in use, the raft was tied next to the pier.

This went on for maybe six months. Sometimes Ben would tow us upstream and we drifted back. At other times, we would resort to carrying it down to the bridge to drift the middle of the estuary, diving off and climbing back onboard.

What a sight! It was like a waterborne trampoline. All the neighbors loved seeing the giant yellow sphere drifting by, boys all over it, jumping and bouncing off, diving under and disappearing into the air pockets that made it look unattended. When tethered alongside the pier, we could jump 10 to 12 feet and bounce clear out of it and into the water.

It stayed floating in the backyard until that fateful day, passing by our pier, we were caught in the five-knot outgoing current and drifted into the superstructure of Fruitvale Bridge, coming close to drowning. Ben, quite angry and worried, had to bring Chiquita to the rescue. Caught in the bridge with the raft collapsing on us, it took full power to pull us to safety. Soon after that, our beloved raft disappeared; no one seemed to know where it had gone. I think by now it's 30 feet down as part of the landfill in Harbor Bay.

In the evenings, at the end of a day's water skiing, with the sun setting, Ben would drop us at the mouth of the San Leandro Bay to swim and drift without life jackets on the outgoing tide, down the middle of the estuary, past the sand and gravel barges, heads bobbing, and boats racing by, under High Street Bridge, past the old ships and pilings. Luckily no one was ever run over.

Back at the Randolph's, we would swim a little while and dive off the huge diving board until half frozen, then into that wonderful hot shower while Ben and Joanie barbecued. Truly a teen paradise!

Who's that Drunk on the Diving Board?

As mentioned earlier, Ben had fished a 14 foot long, 2 by 12 inch wide piece of driftwood out of the estuary and decided to secure it to the end of the pier as a homemade diving board. Depending on the tide, it could be 12 or 14 feet above the water. Too cool!

The board was much different from a normal diving board. When a 180 pound boy hit the end of it, the spring was slower and deeper, but it would catapult us higher and farther than we expected. After the initial test flights and wipeouts, we got the hang of it, and could fly out into deep water, arms spread wide. Some of the minor problems we learned about: low tide, mud bottom, drifting logs, the Chiquita tied to the float below, and the odd droppings from seagulls overhead.

One Sunday, Ben and Joanie had friends arrive by water in their cabin cruiser. They spent the day laughing, eating and towing us kids, as usual, behind the Chiquita. It was such a nice evening, they decided to cruise the San Francisco Bay at sunset, which left maybe five or six of us starving, trustworthy boys behind stuffing ourselves with barbecue, macaroni and potato salads, chips, dip, and whatever else we could find.

Frank had a morning paper route at the time and would pick up and fold his papers at the Alameda Hotel. Somehow he had acquired a quart of Scotch whisky. "Hmmm," we mused. "Let's have a chug-a-lug contest!"

Being a non-drinker, I took one taste and that was enough. The bottle was handed around and around until empty. With all the food and alcohol, stomachs were a little upset, but not Dean's ... he was bombed and began running around doing crazy antics. We started chasing him for fear that he would attract the neighbors' attention. They would surely alert "gentle but fearsome Ben" and there would be repercussions.

Red Dog finally cornered Dean on the end of the diving board, but couldn't get him to come off. So Red, being a little drunk himself, retrieved his dad's handsaw and threatened to cut the board. Dean just kept laughing and taunting the Dog. After maybe ten minutes of this interchange, we were now positive that the neighbors were alerted. Dean didn't quit, so Red followed up on his threat. He sawed clear through the board and Dean, fully clothed while still hugging the wood, had to be dragged from the water.

"Now what?" we asked ourselves.

As Dean was still drunk, I volunteered to drive him home. Dripping wet, I sat him in my front seat and headed for the barn. At the time, my Chevy had straight pipes so I was avoiding cops if possible. I headed down High Street at 10 o'clock on a Sunday evening, and had only one obstacle to get through: the stop sign at High and Encinal, where police would sometimes sit.

As I approached, out of the corner of my eye, I saw my worst fear: a black and white, and me in my well-known maroon and prime, louvered hood, and gold moon hub-capped Chevy, with a wet, drunk passenger. *I'm doomed.*

I took off from the stop sign just sure the officer with X-ray eyes could see the sweat beading up on my forehead and hear my respirations accelerating toward hyperventilation. One block away from the stop, my car sounded like a diesel truck and there was no sign of the police. Two blocks away, car headlights appeared in my mirror; three blocks away, my car illuminated in the most terrifying red glow. No breath mints and a car that smelled like a brewery.

I looked over at a dripping Dean who now seemed to be in a stupor, staring at the floorboards with no reaction to the lights at all. *I'm dead*!

I pulled over to the curb and got out quickly, walking to the rear of my car. Just maybe the cop didn't notice Dean. *Yeah, right.*

Officer Merritt walked up to me, checked my eyes with his flashlight and said, "Hi, Dave … kind of loud. Where are you headed?"

"Home, officer," I replied, with a sheepish grin on my face.

"Who's in the car?" he asked.

Car, what car? "Oh, just a friend. We're on the way home."

He walked over to the passenger door and shined his light in Dean's face; Dean didn't move. He just kept staring at his feet. The officer opened the door and said, "Please step out of the car."

As my life flashed before me, Dean seemed to come to life but, instead of moving out, he slid across to the driver's side, stepped out, staggered around the car past me, and tripped on the curb face-down at the feet of the cop who, at this point, seemed to be about seven feet tall. *Have I mentioned, I'm dead? I must think fast.*

"Officer, we were at a friend's house and Dean showed up drunk! Being a good friend, I'm taking him home," I said.

"Why is he wet?" Officer Merritt asked.

"Uh, he was drunk when I saw him walking down the street and, on the way home, I had to stop at my friend's house, you know, the Randolph's," I explained. "While there, Dean fell off the pier and we had to fish him out. What could I do but try to take him home?"

Oh, that was dumb; I just incriminated Gentle Ben and Joanie while they're still enjoying a night on the bay.

"Honest officer! I haven't been drinking!" I added. "Please let me take him home. I promise you won't see us again tonight."

To my great surprise, he bought the story, let us go with a warning, and even forgot the loud pipe ticket, though he was probably laughing all the way back to the station. I quickly and carefully drove Dean to his house, opened the car door and watched him wobble up the driveway thinking to myself, *Hope he makes it by his dad. Not likely, but maybe he will live after all. No more whiskey! S@# Happens.*

I Could Have Died A Thousand Deaths

The Question is, Could Dave be a Werewolf?

I had just attended the first showing of "I Was a Teenage Werewolf" at the Alameda Theatre, which birthed another great idea: "Let's get some glue and hair from the local costume store and make up as werewolves to scare the girls!"

The glue and hair worked well… until removal time. *There must be a better way.*

Back to the store, where we found clear, form-fitting masks - just the ticket! We created masterpieces and only had to pull them on. We bought cheap silver, synthetic wigs and, with black spray paint, blended the colors.

At that time, a group of 20 to 30 kids from Encinal and Alameda high schools hung out at Ryders Drive-In. The gang of guys and girls would sometimes hike the Oakland Hills at night. (This was before real gangs took over.) We would walk through the trees with flashlights, laughing and talking.

Red Dog and I decided to mess with the group so, one night, bowing out from the romp in the forest, we stayed home… just long enough for me to don my football shoulder pads, Pendleton shirt, werewolf mask, and wig. Then Red drove me up High Street the back way, and into Tilden Park above Skyline Drive, just ahead of the unsuspecting group.

Positioned about 50 feet above the trail and behind a tree, I could hear the gang coming, flashlight in hand. As they got near, I rustled the bushes and heard someone whisper, "Did you hear that?"

The group stopped to listen, and then resumed walking. Again I rustled the bushes, this time peeking out from a bush just long enough for a flashlight beam to hit my face. Then I darted back behind the tree.

A couple of girls screamed and a guy asked, "Did you see that?"

"What?"

"Something crazy up in the trees!"

"Ah, you're seeing things."

This time I moved out into the light, resulting in screams, and a few people started to run. Then the scene changed. The guys got bold and started up the hill, which caused me to run. Soon yours truly, alias the werewolf, was on a dead run downhill, in the dark, in the trees, laughing, with 10 football players in hot pursuit... until I stepped into a two-foot hole and felt my knee crack as I went down in agony.

That night has stayed with me all of my life. You ask why? Well, because of another stupid move, I have had an ACL operation, an orthoscopic procedure, and finally, a full knee replacement. I'm probably the only werewolf in history to go through three surgeries to have the doctors ask, "You were doing *what*?"

Night Cruise to San Francisco

It was another warm fall evening, about 7:00, still about 70 degrees, with a full moon. Ben had left the Chiquita tied to the float thinking it would be used the next day. Red, Budda and Frank owned small, very fast, 11-foot boats with 35-horsepower outboard motors. We used to race up and down the estuary and run through a slough called Sweet Pea at high tide, off San Leandro Bay.

I Could Have Died A Thousand Deaths

"Let's take the boats out for a cruise," one of us suggested.

"Yeah, sounds good," we agreed and cruised toward the Oakland Airport where there was an old ferry boat converted into a restaurant. "Let's tie up, climb the outside, and peer in at the diners. Yeah!" That worked just long enough for the maître d' to give chase. Back to the boats and on to the next adventure.

Budda and Red were in the back, with me in the front cockpit; the boat was almost too heavy. With Flip, Frank, and Heater alongside in Frank's boat, going full speed down the estuary, flying through the warm night air racing each other, I thought, *this feels so good.* Until Frank's engine snapped a shear pin at Jack London Square. Luckily we had another, the fix was done quickly and we were back in business.

Soon we had arrived at the mouth of the San Francisco Bay and were surprised at how calm the water was. Again, being dumb teenagers that are invincible, with no more shear pins aboard, someone said, "Why don't we run over to Fisherman's Wharf and get some crab? It's not that far."

Well, it sounded good at the time to a bunch of imbeciles. No life jackets, dressed only in shorts and T-shirts, black water that could turn and suck us out through the Golden Gate without a trace. No radio, no flares, no one knew where we had gone, and no brains; off we went.

Forty-five minutes later under the Bay Bridge in the dark, someone said, "Ya know, it looks a lot higher than it did from Alameda." We suddenly seemed very small.

"What's that big thing coming at us?" one of the guys yelled.

"The Vallejo Ferry! Look out!"

We took evasive action but couldn't avoid the wake. We hit the waves and were airborne. The boat returned to the water and my knees returned to the ribs of the boat, which was a jarring reminder that I shouldn't have stepped in that hole running through the forest dressed as a werewolf a couple of years back. We almost capsized and I thought to myself again, *we're not in Kansas anymore, Dorothy. My kneecaps hurt and we're getting wet.* But soon we were cruising in the lee of San Francisco Harbor. *It's not so bad,* I reasoned.

Arriving at the Wharf about 9:00 p.m., we climbed up the pier, emerging dripping wet and shivering to the surprise of a group of tourists who didn't see any kind of boat below that could navigate these waters. We walked around for about a half hour and then realized we didn't have the money for crab. We went back to the boat and the thought of a painful ride back across a now daunting waterway on an outgoing tide... *I hope we have enough gas,* I thought apprehensively.

The only silver lining was that there were two boats running together. *Yeah, right.* That lasted for maybe 45 minutes. Now, again under the Bay Bridge, with the wind and waves increasing, the tide against us, the two boats separated and we were in a desperate race to get home before we lost power. *I wonder where the other boat is.*

I Could Have Died A Thousand Deaths

To make any headway we had to keep on a plane, which means we were airborne half the time; my knees were wearing a hole through the bottom of the boat. *I hope we make the channel before I see bilge water*, I agonized.

Now, soaked to the bone with mild hypothermia setting in, I could see the estuary channel marker blinking ahead of us. It seemed to be saying, "Hey, over here!" *Yeah, I see you,* I complained inwardly, *but the tide doesn't want us to get there.*

Two hours into the trip, we passed that blinking light. We made it! *Someday I'll have to write a story called, "Another Day in the Life of Dumb, Dumber, and Associates,"* I thought. I would rather have been home with Mom and brother.

As our heads cleared out of survival mode, we remembered the other boat. Then we heard that wonderful sound of the 35-horse outboard and, out of the shadows, came our wet but smiling trio back home in the channel, alive. *That's enough fun for one night*, I determined. We headed the three miles home to go get something to eat.

Oh, a small detail we forgot: no navigation lights and the possibility of a Coast Guard patrol boat that would love to ticket us.

Heading east with eyes wide open, we saw ahead of us - you guessed it - a bright and shiny Coast Guard cutter coming right at us down the middle of the channel. It didn't look like he had seen us yet, so we decided to separate and move way to the outside edges of the estuary and make a run for it. If we could get past them going 35, we might be able to lose them at the Fruitvale Bridge as they have to wait for it to open, and we could just go under.

Crouched down on the deck, we passed. But they heard the motors in the dark. We saw the floodlights and heard the P.A. system sounding with authority, "This is the Coast Guard! Stop your motors for inspection!"

Yeah, right! We were committed and kept going. The cutter turned, but we were now ahead with maybe a quarter-mile lead. We thought we were fast, but the cutter was gaining. Our only hope was the Fruitvale Bridge. We crossed under the Park Street Bridge, with only one more to go, but the cutter was maybe an eighth of a mile away and closing.

Looking ahead now, we saw the Fruitvale. I couldn't believe my eyes! It was starting to open! Those dirty rats on the cutter must have radioed the bridge. Under the bridge, now only 10 houses from home, the cutter was still waiting. What do we do?

Red thought quick as he saw the Chiquita in the water. "Let's see if we can get the two smaller boats on the lift!" he said.

They fit and started to rise, just as the cutter cleared the Fruitvale Bridge. "Everybody duck and hold your breath!" We could only hope that Ben and Joanie stayed in the house watching television.

The cutter passed slowly, floodlights scouring the piers. I must have held my breath for two minutes while it continued down through High Street. Then they returned, leaving the scene after having lost the objects of their pursuit.

No harm, no foul, no brains, no loss of life, no remorse, no return to San Francisco by small boat. *Mom never knew.*

I Could Have Died A Thousand Deaths

The Prototype Skateboard

We were in need of a new challenge. Someone remembered the old orange crate coasters we built as kids. Why didn't we improve on that concept? Let's take an old 2x4" stud and some steel shoe skates, merge them, and try balancing.

Well it kind of worked, but there were no hills in Alameda, so off we went to the Oakland Hills. Instead of a gradual hill, of course we went straight to Joaquin Miller Park. Big mistake. Gravity does work but not always to one's benefit, as flatlanders would soon find out. At that time in history, bloody, holey Levis were not in vogue. Mom, on our meager budget, had to buy new pants for her stupid teenager; we decided to let someone in later years develop a better skateboard.

The Coaster

Not done with the hills quite yet, we started a new project in Budda's garage: four soap box derby wheels, some plywood shaped onto a 2'x4' platform with a 1"x2" trim piece around the front and two sides, an apple crate backrest, and rope steering. Looked great! The only problem was that we tired easily pushing our creation on flat streets. *Hmmm, maybe the Oakland Hills would work better.* Redwood Road, here we come. Dean got his dad's truck (hotwired or legal, I'm not sure). Off to the hills. *What fun!*

At the top of Skyline and Redwood Road, we decided, "If we go one at a time on the coaster, it'll take all day. Why not try two?"

Budda sat in the back with the rope steering in hand, then Red sat down between his legs. That looked good … but wait, maybe three could fit, so I, having donned my football helmet (as if that would make any difference), slipped between Red's legs. We were ready!

Looking back now, it's hard to believe we were that stupid. The picture, again, is three senseless 170 pound boys sitting on a 2'x4' piece of ply with ball bearing wheels, between each other's legs, my heels hooked over the lip of the coaster, toes extending off the front, knees in my chest. *Oh crap, has anyone thought to install brakes?* Not!

At that moment, we let go and gravity took over. Dean and the guys were following at first, but then we started to pull away. Dean said later that we were separating at about 50 miles per hour. Coming into the first turn, centrifugal force took over. I knew we had made a big miscalculation; we were in the oncoming lane and, when Budda tried to pull us back, we went up on two wheels.

I saw a car coming toward us and we couldn't do anything but careen toward them. Luckily, they saw us and ran off the road, or I would have been facemask-to-grill, buried in an auto wrecking yard instead of a graveyard.

Budda got us back on the right side of the road. But then I saw an oak tree the size of a four-story building rapidly approaching and thought, *I really, really love my life... What do you know, we made it!* Next I thought, as we careened past the two big turns, *What's ahead?* Big Bear Bar and Store with all kinds of cars not really looking for three nuts, six inches off the ground, nearing the speed of sound with very little steering, no horn, no brakes, no toilet paper, and no sense. Another deep breath as we passed by.

Out of the corner of my eye, I saw three people with the strangest looks on their faces, as if they couldn't believe what they were spotting: three boys sitting between each other's legs, floating somewhere between 60 and Mach one. As fast as their eyes focused and their brain perceived, we disappeared around the corner and they were not sure what they just observed.

Again, as I had time to think, I was relieved that no slow moving cars were in front of us, I would have become the first five-mile-an-hour impact bumper before they had been invented. Soon we began to slow and Dean caught up with us. We were heroes for the day.

Later, others tried the steeper side of Skyline by Devil's Punch Bowl and beat our speed record while I drove the truck. Finally, we tried the reverse direction on Redwood Road which was more twisting, and our truck soon fell behind. Coming around a turn, we met an oncoming car; the driver, a woman, was looking back with a terrified expression. *That's not a good sign!*

Rounding the turn, I saw Budda before me, lying face down on the white line, that lovely 2'x4' platform with shiny, red ball bearing wheels free spinning in the bright morning sun. Heater was lying semiconscious, face up in the ditch, and Red was 100 yards ahead, his nose redder than his hair, hugging his knee and rocking back and forth in great pain.

Apparently, the speed and the tight turns had gotten the best of Budda's steering ability. Rounding a turn into the oncoming lane, they came face to face with that car, veered back into their lane, and centrifugal force had its way. As the coaster lifted into the air, Red flew off the front, trying to run at somewhere near 55 miles an hour. Now Red was lean and fast, but not that fast. Picture the Roadrunner, legs spinning, but body gaining ground until, eventually, he made a three point landing, nose and knees. Heater was groaning, "How did I get in the ditch?"

And Budda was mumbling, "I've never tasted white line before. Why is the coaster riding me?"

I don't know what happened to the coaster after we hung it in Budda's garage, but we lived - somewhat scarred up - to adventure yet another day.

Cars and Cliffs

Devil's Punch Bowl was an old rock quarry we passed on the way up to Skyline Drive. We often hiked through the trees and brush, and would climb down inside, just for the adventure. One of my neighbors gave me an old Pontiac that didn't run. *Maybe I can fix it.* After a while I was bored with it, so the Shifters put their heads together and decided to tow it up to the Punch Bowl and shove it off a 500 foot drop (having seen one too many movies about cars crashing over cliffs). We towed it through Castro Valley to the fire trail and up the back side of the hill to the cliff. With one giant push, we had our own movie spectacular. *That didn't take long.* Two days later, Mom received a knock at the door by the Oakland Police. It seems that they had investigated the wreck, concerned that someone might be dead inside. My neighbor's name was still on the title, but Mom had to pay the tow bill to remove our movie prop. *Sorry Mom!*

Smokin' Opel

Gary had a foreign car, an Opel with a small block V-8. By loosening the rear brake shoes, he could lock the front brakes, rev the engine, pop the clutch, and smoke the tires for long periods of time. By keeping pressure on the front brakes, the car would move slowly but the tires would keep spinning. The only real problem was tire cost; Gary could burn the tires off in a couple of days. We would buy cheap tires at the auto wreckers, knowing that they'd only last a short time. It didn't matter if the cord was showing on the side wall as long as they had good tread. We didn't think safety; we weren't going fast, just leaving tire tracks all over town.

One day, with a car full of guys, he started his burnout from the front of Alameda High; he burned to the corner and continued at right turns, onto Oak Street, and out of sight. When he performed this burning of tires, the smoke would enter the car through holes in the floorboard and fender wells. I was in Ryders Drive-In when Gary's car arrived straight from a great display of black rubber on asphalt. The smoke in the car was so thick, you couldn't see anyone inside. They skidded to a halt; four doors flew open, smoke exploding from all sides. Out of the cloud stepped four proud, laughing, choking, coughing, teary-eyed Shifters, to the amazement of the bystanders!

Can a '49 Chevy Jump a Telephone Pole?

Dick Stevens worked full time at the corner Chevron station. His main car, until it met a brick wall at the end of Flower Lane, was a '47 Ford convertible powered by Oldsmobile. After that mishap, Dick was given a '49 Chevy four-door sedan. With nothing better to do, we used to ride around town.

One day Dick, Red, Budda, Flip, Frank and I were cruising the back streets when Dick said, "Ya know, these Chevy transmissions are strong. I wonder, if I were to ram the car into reverse at 35, could it burn rubber backwards?"

"Do it!" came the cry in unison.

So Dick did, and the car did, though I bounced off the dashboard. The result was a cloud of tire smoke, a few turned heads, and the prettiest U-shaped burn pattern on the asphalt. All around town for the next couple of weeks there appeared U-shaped burn marks, especially on Lincoln. Many questions from the public were never answered.

Winter was in full swing and we decided that the open fields at the west end of town were perfect for spinning donuts in the mud and tall grass. It would have worked even better if we had walked the field first to see what was in the tall grass, but not us.

Problem one: we entered at our normal speed of 35 mph, and promptly went airborne, having jumped a concrete foundation. No harm, no foul: the car was still in one piece as we spun in the mud, slipping and sliding to a stop.

Problem two: we were now inside and needed to leave. The only way out was to jump a horizontal telephone pole that was there to keep cars out.

Dick accelerated to launch speed and hoped for the best. As the Chevy and five bobble heads went flying, we were getting used to impacts and were better able to ride with, instead of against, the dashboard. With a crash, the car bottomed out back onto terra firma, and off for the station, slowing just long enough to hit reverse and spin on the wet road. We soon grew bored with spinning U's and decided to drive the top of the Bay Farm Island dike which made an S turn, gravel flying in all directions. By that time, we had lost all the hubcaps. Most of the chrome was off or sticking out at odd angles.

Dave, Red Dick and Flip

Stopping at my house on Beach Road one afternoon, we robbed the refrigerator and, returning to the car with most of us inside, Flip ran up onto the hood, then onto the roof, which collapsed down on our heads making the doors hard to open. A quick thrust upward and the roof returned.

"Hey! Why not take a picture of four of us standing on the roof?"

"Hey! Wouldn't it be cool if we chopped a hole in the roof with my pick?"

"Let's do it!"

From that experience, we learned that we could drive through town with or without the roof collapsed. Anything to get attention.

Alameda Police once pulled us over for a safety check. The cop was concerned that some of the chrome was sticking out too far and could impale a pedestrian, so we obliged by pulling the offending chrome off and he let us go with a smile and warning. Driving from the island to the mainland, we passed that infamous concrete wall that I would be writing about 56 years later, separating the road from the golf course. At that time, the wall was much higher as the road bed was lower. If you stand on the golf course side today, you will see what I mean.

"Why not drive up against the wall after dark and see if we can makes sparks?"

We drove and drove that night, sparks flying, a real light show - until we realized we had worn clear through the wrap-around bumper and ground down the fender endangering the tire. From there, back to the mud fields by this time, and one too many jumps, we broke the suspension. It was Sunday night. All the wreckers were closed and the car had burned its last U.

We parked old Bessie out in front of the wreckers, started the engine, put a large rock on the gas pedal, and let it run wide open, thinking it would blow up. Thirty minutes later, the Chevy was still screaming, though the sound would change at times. It was smoking more but there was no sign of explosion.

We bowed our heads and gave her the last rights, said our final goodbyes, and left her at full throttle.

Utah State's Homecoming Game

It was 1966 and Brother Jim had a full ride scholarship to Utah State University in Logan. Mom and I decided to take the long weekend and race eleven hours across Nevada. At that time, with no speed limit to restrain Mom's '65 Pontiac Bonneville, we could catch his last homecoming game.

Thinking back to four years earlier, I had visited Salt Lake in my '32 Ford roadster on her shakedown trip. I had dreamt of a trip of this sort since the debut of "Route 66" on television in October of

I Could Have Died A Thousand Deaths

1960. At that time the '32 was still in pieces, but the dream kept me going day and night.

In 1962, the car now on four wheels sporting a convertible top, Shifters plaque, chrome everywhere, fat tires, headers, and that 24 coats of pearlescent blue lacquer, with a candy apple red racing stripe, and gold pin striping. All it needed was a full tank of gas. John, my neighbor, and I had decided to travel cross country and live our dream. Sunday night about eight, looking forward to the Monday morning departure, John approached me in the garage while putting last minute touches on my creation.

"Dave?"

"Yeah, what's going on?"

With a sheepish look he said, "Something's come up. I can't go."

"You mean you're chickening out! Too bad, but I'm leaving at 7:00 a.m. if you change your mind."

Looking back it was a gutsy thing to do, with very little money, no spare tire or tow service, and no side windows in a state that has

Entering the Salt Flats

summer rain. Call it blind faith. *Now I would call it a little unwise.* I stayed in Reno the first night, Wendover the second, Salt Lake the third, on my way to visit cousins in Nebraska. In Salt Lake I found a semi-secure motel, showered, donned my best Levis and Pendleton to cruise down the boulevard feeling, oh, so cool.

There it was, a glorious sphere of light and life, the local drive-in all lit up in neon and tail lights, encircled with cars and car hops, not knowing they were waiting for the cool rod from California. Pulling up to a stall almost center in the circle, I let the '55 Olds Rocket 88 engine throb just long enough to turn heads, a slight rev so as to hear the ¾ cam, solid lifters, light aluminum Schafer fly wheel, then silence. I had them looking, and car hops responded. I'm living a Hollywood dream, the perfect movie... *and I'm James Dean.*

There were a couple of waves and nods from the locals, though a little too cool to come over and talk. I downed my burger, fries and cherry Coke, then paid the bill leaving a larger than needed tip for the voluptuous blonde waitress. I hit the starter, and 400 horses roared to life, heads turned trying not to be too impressed, but they were. A flip of the switches on the black walnut dashboard and into reverse as the custom speed shop headlights played off of a '56 Chevy to the right of me. Waiting to enter South Temple, the radio came on while "In the Still of the Night" was playing, a rev of the engine, just enough to hear that glorious sound of the glass pack mufflers, as my 1950 Pontiac taillights fade into the night. Three blocks up the boulevard, sitting at a red light, I heard the rumble of a maroon '34 Ford coupe pulling up next to me, another rev, and I knew his meaning. In the coupe is a face looking my way with a grin that says,

1934 Ford

"You wanna go?"

No need to reply; he knew my answer. A green light, then smoke in the night. *Not a problem; he's toast!* As I waited at the next red light, he had had enough and motioned me to the curb.

"Hi. My name's Jim! What've you got in that thing?" he asked while stepping out of the coupe.

"Olds," I said. "How about you?"

"Chevy. I thought I was fast, but you're the man. I need more speed equipment; it's hard to find in Salt Lake. What's your name?"

"Dave."

"What are you doing in town?" he questioned.

"Traveling through to Nebraska to visit family," I responded.

"How long are you staying here?"

"I was leaving tomorrow."

Jim looked disappointed, "Too bad! Our "Monarchs" car club meets on Wednesday. I sure would like a "Shifter" from California at the meeting. You could stay at our president's house. I know he has room."

"Sounds interesting," I pondered.

Jim said, "I'll pick you up tomorrow morning and we'll go over to his house."

Monday morning we met John and his show quality '27 T truck.

John invited me to stay and said, "Let's go camping in the White Mountains just up there. I've been wanting to go since I arrived from L.A. five years ago. I hear there's a cave called Neffs. It's supposed to be the deepest in the western hemisphere and, with you here, we have a good enough reason. We'll be back for the Wednesday meeting, then you can leave on Thursday."

"Sounds like fun," I agreed.

To shorten the story, we went, we found the cave, climbed down about 500 feet, almost fell the other 500 and, with flashlight batteries depleted, groped for the cave entrance vowing never to do that again.

Back in the city and one race too many, I had blown second gear in my '39 Cadillac transmission. I met two guys from Oklahoma, Ed and Don, working at the Mobil station hoping they would have a lead on a second gear. Now I'm in big trouble, with a crippled

Being Towed Home

transmission, 800 miles from home. The guys had the neatest red '40 Ford coupe with a '56 T-bird engine. *What am I going to do?*

Don said, "Hey, Dave! We've never been to California. What do you say we tow you home? All you have to do is pay for food and gas. We'll drive straight through and see the west as we go."

"Really? Great!" I responded enthusiastically.

"We'll leave Friday and have the long weekend to get back," Ed chimed in.

With my duce in tow behind the '40, we left Friday night and arrived home at noon Saturday. Mom fixed lunch, Ed and Don said good-bye, and I never saw them again.

I Could Have Died A Thousand Deaths

Now back in 1966, Mom and I have made it to Salt Lake with only 60 miles to Logan, and we will see Brother Jim play football. We pulled into the nearest gas station. The attendant responded with, "Can I help you?"

"Fill 'er up with Custom 104." Thinking back to my time there, I asked, "Have you heard of the 'Monarchs' Car Club?"

Can you believe it? A city of close to a million people, and the guy responded, "Yeah, I used to be a member, but they changed their name a few year ago to 'Shifters Midwest.'"

"What did you say?" I asked in total disbelief.

"Shifters. Not sure why, but it stuck."

Hmm, this sounds like a screen play, but nobody would believe it.

Shifters Reunion - 2012

It's time again for a Shifters of Alameda car club reunion. So much time has passed. It doesn't seem possible but, as I look back in my scrapbook, I am privileged beyond measure to think of the life and friends God has given me in a city called Alameda.

Fifty-eight years later, there's no pickup truck, no '49 Merc or Chevy, no louvered hood or moon hubcaps. There's just Dean and Joanne, Freddy (alias the Fonz), Bev, Ken, Carl, Judy, Jim, John, Laurence, Tom, Tubby and Marlene - now driving their motor homes - and me in a Toyota pickup. *Did I say boring?*

We are now truly seniors: Red Dog and Frank are gone; Flip just recently died lying under his '56 Chevy. Budda can't make it to the reunion; Heater showed up with his younger brother, Tom, in a nice Chevy-powered '47 custom, which makes our day.

My Life's Work Begins

Through all the Shifters adventures and my work experiences, I was apprenticing in my future career. My big break came when I became an Operating Engineer, leaving the filling station behind. I was hired by Peterson Tractor, the Caterpillar dealer for Northern California. At Peterson I steam cleaned, sand blasted, and painted tractors, which gave me the chance to drive every type of Cat and Letourneau equipment from brand new back to the early Twentieth Century. Eventually I received a Class A driver's license with a heavy equipment certificate. I was assigned the job of loading the

Tandem 657s Earthmovers

overweight, over-height equipment to be trucked to various construction sites. If the earthmovers were too big for a trailer, I would drive them with pilot cars to be delivered to the California Aqueduct project in the San Joaquin Valley. I also tested experimental equipment being readied for production. After passing the Alameda Fire Department test, I had to choose between being foreman of used equipment or the fire department. I took a cut in pay but made the right choice.

My first home after joining the AFD was at 911 Lilac Street on BFI. Three years later in 1972, with the help of Harry and his moving van, the family moved to my coveted home at 3019 Marina Drive that had previously belonged to the Randolph family. Larry, Pete, Bob and Gary, Moe and Bob, and another half-dozen guys that should be remembered, moved the whole house in two hours and we were breaking bread by 11:00 a.m. Only in the fire department would teamwork and friendship join in such a way. We lived there on the Alameda Oakland Estuary for six years. I had spent my teenage years waterskiing and boating along the channel and now we got that same wonderful home for $42,000. I spent my days off rebuilding our pier, and later the neighbors' piers, for extra money. I learned the waterfront like the back of my hand. It served me and the fire department well in later years teaching fireboat handling and waterfront familiarization. Living on the channel, most of the fire crews found themselves pulling up in the boat for a visit whenever they were out training. My kids and the neighbors loved to see the guys arrive to inspect my work and consume a Coke. At times my good friend, Dave, and his family would paddle into the backyard on their kayak for a visit. Dave always did his job well. I'm sure by now he's logged 100,000 miles on his bicycle between Hanson and Main, Marina and Beach, killed a million tennis balls, and strung a thousand rackets. Not to mention the number one service for Alameda Fire Department, a pictorial record of our history. Thanks, Dave!

And then there was another Dave, by the name of Burton, *a friend who sticks closer than a brother,* **Proverbs 18:24.** He would often visit the station, especially on Christmas or New Year's evenings with his two daughters, Michelle and Emily. He would bring a bottle of sparkling cider, knowing that I was missing the family times. God bless you, brother David!

Dad and Brother Jim 1947

255 Beach Road

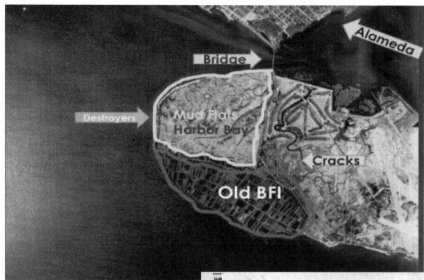

Fish could be caught by hand

I Could Have Died A Thousand Deaths

Freemont Drag Strip
Brother Jim in the car

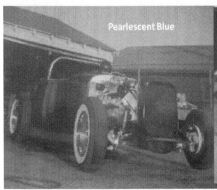

Pearlescent Blue

Mustang Red

Testing the Tandem D9's

I Could Have Died A Thousand Deaths

Sheep's Foot Compactor

Testing the Tandem 657 Earthmover

55 Pontiac, Corvette Eater

51 Olds

Brother Jim
Houston Oilers

?? Budda, Red Dog, Heater, Frank

PART THREE

The Fire Years - One Man's Perspective

*I see him crawling out of the building, steam rising
from his turnout coat and a smile on his face. I know that
I'm in the company of men of uncommon valor.*

Alameda Fire Department - Saturday, October 16, 2004

Last night, Patty and I attended the movie, "Ladder 49." What fun!
On the same day my neighbor loaned me the book, "Firehouse" by
David Habersham, the story of Engine 40 and Ladder 35 that lost
12 men on 9/11 in New York. As I read of these brave men and

64

then reviewed the movie that night, I realized that Bertha had loaned me her book and suggested that we see the movie 36 years to the day I entered the Alameda Fire Department to start my career. I had been dabbling in writing for a while but am now inspired to tell of my wonderful life experience and to honor so many of my brothers and one sister that I shared 25 years of life with. That night after the movie my thoughts went back those 36 years to the start of my career...

In the Beginning

Webb Avenue, Old Station One, Circa 1890's

I'm 27 years old, with ten years in the trades. I left a well-paying job as a heavy equipment operator, demonstrator. Six months of

competitive testing and I'm starting over at Station One in the 2400 block of Webb Avenue, Alameda, California. This old station was built pre-1900. I have many pictures from my dad's great collection of horse-drawn rigs standing in the three arched wooden doorways of this station; these same coil-spring-activated doors are now stretched open to welcome the five of us into our future. The recruits are starting a month of on-the-job training before being assigned to our shifts and stations. The new kids this go-around are: Vince, Larry, Minor, Dave, and me.

The apparatus room interior is probably 25 feet high, and contains two font line rigs and two reserves following. The smell of smoke, gasoline, solvent, and old wood greet you as you step through the door. It feels as if you are stepping back a hundred years in time. The rigs are different but the station is the same. To the right front corner, a black steel spiral staircase ascends to the second floor library and dorms. That spiral staircase now stands in the Elks Club on Santa Clara Avenue. On the west wall is a rack of spare 50 foot rolls of hose. Above the racks hang turnout coats and helmets. To the east sits the chief's car and the resuscitator wagon. Directly behind them is a windowed cubical with the officer's desk. Next to the cubical sits the station Gamewell Alarm System, pegboard, dispatch radios, maps of the city, and hydrant locations, enclosed only by an oak railing and gate that separates dispatch from the main apparatus room. Assorted oak captain's chairs, as old as the stations, have been reinforced with wire to hold them together after years of being

Monk Morgan's Chair

tilted back on two legs. These chairs are neatly lined up against the railing. To enter that area, we must pass through the oak gate, then left, to the officer's cubicle or right, to the switchboard phone system, manned 24 hours a day.

Out from the gate, left of center, sits a wonderful brass pole. The pole brought back memories of 1946 with my mom, brother Jim,

and me standing at that railing, waiting to see Dad, and hearing the dispatcher call for him, "Hey Jackson, ya got visitors!" (Jackson was Dad's nickname). And then seeing him descend the pole with a grin that came from a man who truly loved what he was doing, and loved the family visits as much as I did. **He was my hero.**

Behind the pole was a long staircase clad in period wooden, beadboard paneling with a landing half-way up that reversed direction 180 degrees, then up through the ceiling to join a short hallway and two doors. Left to the kitchen and straight to the dormitories. Under the stairway was the private phone, storage and turnout equipment room. Below in the basement was the boiler room for station heating. I am told that, in the days of the horse-drawn steamers, hot water was circulated from the boiler through the rig's heating coils to keep the water near operating temperature. The water, then, could be brought up to steam quickly en route to the fire. To the rear, was another set of large, arched doors leading to the shop and hose drying tower. Gus, the city mechanic, ruled this space full of parts, tools, paint, and history. In the floor was a pit that had seen almost a 125 years of undercarriages, from steamers to gasoline rigs, and hard rubber to pneumatic tires.

The kitchen was a patchwork of history: oldest... old... not so old, and in need of renovation. One long table, in the center of the room with a skylight overhead, a stove on the east wall, a refrigerator to the north, and counters on the west. On the south wall, a sink and door to the outside balcony, next to the hose-drying tower, and stairs to the backyard. On the wall under the table, was a fireman's worst nightmare: one duplex outlet with a half dozen plugs and extension cords overloading a single circuit. Do you think there could be pennies in the fuse box? Nah! *Only in a fire station*, I thought.

A cribbage board and a couple of decks of cards, with the edges bent and frayed from years of shuffling, were ready for a game. Ashtrays were everywhere as probably 90 percent of the men smoked. Upon entering the dorm, you could see wooden bead-board and plaster walls painted a blah cream color, many single

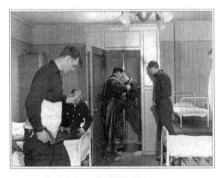

beds with iron headboards. My mind returns to a picture I have of Dad, in bed reading a magazine, a cigarette in his mouth, his hat tilted jauntily to one side as they did in the 40's. *How times have changed.* To the west was the bathroom and left center was a closet door that opened to a cubicle that enclosed access to that wonderful brass pole.

To look down would take your breath away, as the floor opened to see the concrete of the apparatus room below. At first it was a little unnerving to reach for the pole. But, then, to see John Hales, Sr. run across the room, bells ringing, him yelling,

"AH--OOOO--GAAAH, AH--OOOO--GAAAH," and hit the pole with such force that the brass would seem to ripple and flex from ceiling to floor. Then he would disappear like the contents of a public air-assisted toilet. **Now you see him, now you don't.** Standing below, you knew who was on the pole, and you stayed clear. Then came Jack Reason, often sliding upside down in full control. Jack was amazing at fires; he was kind of like a Tasmanian devil. You didn't get in his way; just let him go and take some of the credit.

At the bottom, the pole and the stairs converge dangerously close; if the men were not careful, a serious collision could happen. To the front of the dorm, through the locker room, were windows facing Webb Avenue. You would turn left to the study, or right to the assistant chief's rooms. To the left rear of the dorm was the bathroom and lieutenant's room, or right rear to the captain's room.

From the front windows you had a great view of the street below. A story told by Moe goes something like this: Jack bet Harry that he could hide inside the station and Harry wouldn't be able to find him. The bet was on. Jack went to the second floor front room, raised the wooden blinds, and lowered the top of a double-hung window down alongside the bottom pane. He then stepped up and perched in the frame on the two widows, and pulled the blinds halfway down. To walk into the room, you could look out the lower widow to see the street below and never realize that Jack was just above you, chuckling. From outside looking up, he raised quite a ruckus as people thought a fireman had finely snapped and was going to jump. Meanwhile, inside, Harry combed the whole station with frustration but no results. Jack won the bet.

I Could Have Died A Thousand Deaths

At around age 16, passing by Station One on my way home from football practice, I would stop at Tucker's Ice Cream on the corner of Park Street and Webb Avenue. Looking down the street, I would hope that the apparatus room doors were standing open, and that some of my surrogate fathers were on duty. Chairs were always occupied and, of course, tilted back. One of my dreams was to master the tilt, which I eventually did. I only stood watch one night behind that oak railing as this station was to be closed by the end of the month, December of 1968.

We were not allowed to sleep through the night while on watch, but could sit in an old oak recliner. As I sat in that recliner, my part of the room was illuminated by a 60 watt bulb. Moving out from the watch area, the light dimmed into the shadows of the surrounding apparatus room. The smell was incredible. I was alone downstairs, but everything seemed to be moving. A cold breeze leaked through the non-insolated walls. With the pipes clinking, and an occasional creaking of floorboards from above, I was glad my back was to the wall. The building was alive with sounds that couldn't be heard during the day. The light coming through the windows from passing cars played tricks with the shadows. The ghost of Monk Morgan, the only Alameda firefighter to die in a station on duty, moved among the rigs. And there I sat, in the spotlight behind that gate. I could feel the spirits of so many that had gone before. And now, as I write this story in 2015, I am but a memory, a name in the history books. Maybe a good story will be told, or a laugh about how anal I was. I ate, slept, and dreamt of the AFD from age 3 to 27. I lived the AFD from 1968-1994, and will remember until I die that we had purpose.

*I was in the right place at the right time,
had the right friends,
and did the right service for the community.
We truly had the right stuff.*

First Day on the Job

October 15, 1968, 7:30 a.m.

I'm very nervous as I begin to merge my life with 125 years of Alameda Fire Department history. Surrounded by two shifts of guys, I see Frank at the table. He pulls out a cigar, with ritual-like purpose and great savor, unwraps and smells it, looks with great admiration, pauses until everyone is watching. Then, with the fury of a steel bear trap, takes a big bite and starts to chew. Frank looks over at a new guy that's pretty nervous and says, "Hey kid, pour yourself a cup of coffee, grab a chair and sit down for 25 years or so."

At 0800, we are introduced to calisthenics the AFD way. In full uniform, we form a circle with the lieutenant leading. Harry is noticeable, immediately behind, and partially out of sight of the

officer. He had put down his cigar and was smiling and running in place without his toes ever leaving the ground, a truly amazing feat indeed.

Every day we would attend the Training Center for hose lays, tactics and strategy, ladder drill, and assorted tool training. We would visit one of the four stations, with our goal being to learn, in one month, every piece of equipment on all seven rigs and two ambulances.

This, again, reminds me of an anomaly with the two Porta-Powers on Trucks 1 and 2. We were to read and memorize the equipment from the training manual, learning to use them. Having come from a trade that used 40 ton Porta-Powers on 100 ton earth movers, I thought to compare our two Porta-Powers. From first look, they seemed exactly the same. The Fire Department Manual, however, said there was an inconsistency between them. Truck 1 had a 10 inch extension, while Truck 2 had a 9 inch. As I looked at them fully extended, you could see that Truck 1 had the numbers 1 through 10 stamped on the shaft, with the 10 barely showing as it entered the cylinder. On Truck 2's, it numbered 1 through 9 with no 10 showing, but with another inch of travel left. When I took a ruler to each, their extensions measured exactly the same. In manufacturing, the number 10 must have been left off, which is no big deal, except to the training officer who thought he had a nugget to catch us on. This has to go down in history as the height of stupidity, someone in the far distant past that shouldn't have been in charge of equipment made a command decision and said there was an inch difference, apparently because he couldn't see the 10. Tradition!

Do you think I could get the training officer to correct the error? No, I was ignored as a new kid. It took me more than 10 years to personally challenge and bring about the correction. I finally won out. Traditions are good but sometimes blind us. By now Porta-Powers have been replaced by the Jaws of Life and it doesn't matter to anyone but me.

The five of us entered our training month together. The routine was to arrive at Station One by 7:30 a.m. At change of shift, we helped the regular crew clean from the previous day, then checked over the apparatus and all equipment. At 8:30 a.m., the Gamewell Alarm was tested with three rounds of three bells, then a radio check, in which Central would tone the radios, and all apparatus operators would acknowledge Central. After radio check, we gathered in the dayroom for coffee and the rundown of our day's training. We would be picked up about 9:30 by whichever engine or truck was going to the Training Center.

At the Training Center, we would pull and connect hose, raise ladders, and mainly do hands on until 11:30, then back to Station One for lunch. At 1:00, we would go back to the Training Center for the afternoon, or to a class at one of our four stations. This accomplished many things; we met most of the men in the department while they met and were sizing up their new batch of kids.

I soon realized that I was with a large group of interesting and, in most cases, talented guys. The five of us worked hard to prove ourselves and to be accepted. The routine was often broken by an alarm; we stopped whatever we were doing and watched the crew swing into action. As we newer guys stood out of the way, that feeling that I had when I was four, sitting on my tricycle, watching Dad go by on Engine Three, came flooding back, "I want to go too." To this day, the sound of a siren takes me back.

Our First Rescue

Alameda Training Center - Mecartney Road, 10:00 a.m.

It's about three weeks into our training and, again, we're raising ground ladders at the Training Center. We heard a car crash into the concrete wall that separates Mecartney Road and the training grounds. That wall that I knew so well was seven feet tall from our

73

side but, on the other side, it was only about five feet to the roadway. As we looked toward the sound of the crash, we could see that a fast-moving car had entered the turn, glancing off the wall. I didn't know until later that the passenger, a girl, had grabbed the wheel in hopes of stopping the car. We ran to the wall and I stepped up on the ledge which put my head above the wall. The right door was opened and we could see her fall out. The car continued on. As it passed, I could see the man inside. I looked right, and saw the girl staggering toward me; she seemed to be crying. I hurdled the wall and ran to her. She collapsed, crying, "He was trying to rape me!"

I carried her to the training tower and yelled, "Call the cops to blockade the bridge!"

I knew there was no other way off the island. While the guys comforted her, I ran back to the wall knowing he had to pass by again to make his escape. As he passed, we got a good look but had no way to apprehend him. He beat the police to the bridge, but we had the license plate number and he was soon caught. One year later, I received a summons to appear in Superior Court to testify on her behalf. The Defense Attorney was pretty smug; he had been to the scene, stood at our location, and realized that we could not see over the seven foot wall from the ground. I was called to the stand, face to face with the assailant.

The attorney proceeded to attack. "Mr. LeMoine, your testimony says that you saw my client and could identify him."

"Yes," I answered.

"Then, can you tell me how a man of six feet could see over a seven foot wall?" With a slight smile, he was sure he had me.

I looked at the assailant and then to him and, with satisfaction, I answered, "Sir, from the age of seven I lived on Bay Farm Island. At least twice a week while growing up, my friends and I would climb and walk on that wall. If you had looked a little closer, you would have noticed that there is a ledge to step up on, which puts a man of six feet at least twelve inches above the wall. The road bed on the other side is only five feet below the top of the wall. We heard the crash and ran to the wall. Knowing the ledge was there, I stepped up and was easily able to see him pass by. Because of the impact with the wall, he was still on our side of the road and maybe six feet from me. Again, as he returned and passed by, we had a second chance to see him. By then, there were five of us looking on. There is no doubt in my mind that he is that man."

The attorney said, "No further questions. You may step down." With a smile and a feeling of great satisfaction, I left for home and the assailant left for the penitentiary.

My Baby Boy is not Breathing!

Station One, 1984, 6:00 a.m.

The call: the report of a two year old boy not breathing. On arrival, we enter the apartment to see a mother by the crib with a two year old in her arms. The father is just standing there, presumably in shock. She says, "My boy was okay an hour ago."

He is still warm and has some color. No ambulance is near, so Captain Steckler makes a tough decision, knowing the hospital is only ten blocks away. He will drive and I will do CPR in the cab of Engine Three on the way to the hospital. I scoop up the baby and into the cab we go; I'm getting a good breath exchange as we race through the cool morning air toward the hospital. His color is holding. As we pull in front of Alameda Emergency, the nurses take him from me and move into a trauma room. My job is done in a matter of a half hour. We have gone from sleeping, to racing through town, to mouth-to-mouth, to the nurses, to nothing. What kind of a job is this? I know the doctor did everything possible for close to an hour. With tears and a look of resignation he says, "That's all I can do," and pronounces him dead. Lying quietly on the table, the boy looks so healthy. What could have gone wrong? Only God can answer that. We did the best we could but it wasn't enough. Next time we must do better.

Hey Guys! My House is on Fire!
Station One, 1976, 11:00 a.m.

Our home was on Marina Drive near the east end of town. I was driving Engine One, with Bob driving Truck One. Mid-morning we heard the still horn, the usual first sound to alert us of a call coming in. I hurried to the front room and asked Bill Simeon, the dispatcher, for the address: "3019 Marina Drive; a house fire."

I paused in disbelief with a gasp. "That's my house! That's my house! Hey guys, my house is on fire!"

We broke all records leaving the station. This time I knew that I burned rubber out of the apparatus room down Encinal, left on Broadway, accelerating through Central and Santa Clara. I'm frantically thinking, *what's burning and where is my family?* By this time the guys on the tailboard must have lost their footing and were holding on with just their hands, flapping in the draft of the engine as I broke all the rules. Further down Central, Truck 1 was so close I could see Bob's face in my mirror. I thought to myself again, *What's burning? Where are my wife and two little girls?*

76

Right turn onto Fernside, the engine was flat out as we reached Harvard. I slowed to 1800 RPM's and the five speed slipped smoothly into fourth and then third. I turned left two short blocks and right, onto Marina. As we pulled up in front, we could see Laura and the girls standing on the lawn of our house, safe. I breathed a sigh of relief. I've never seen the guys move so fast. The fire turned out to be small, behind the dryer, with lots of smoke damage. I was grateful to Laura for her care of the children, and a bit chagrined about the fire. I know firsthand what it feels like to be on the other side for a change.

A Slight Hint of Horse Manure

Station Two, Engine Two, Truck Two, & Resuscitator Wagon

This station is at 635 Pacific Avenue, at the west end of town (before renovation). On approach, you see a double over-head apparatus room door; I still have a picture in my mind of my childhood, standing next to the only tiller truck in our history until the arrival of two new monster trucks in 2014. The old Seagraves truck with an aerial ladder was raised under spring power, while the platform rotated and the ladder extended manually by the men on the turntable using large crank wheels. Truck Two was probably the best part of the show during Fire Prevention Week at our drill tower. To the right, the office windows, front door and dayroom windows. Upon entering the front door, the hallway extended all the way to the rear and into the kitchen. You detected the smell of wood, brass polish, smoke, floor wax, diesel fuel and maybe, just maybe, a slight hint of horse manure. To the left was the office; next, the turnout and phone room; left again is a short hallway, bath, and apparatus room door; or straight again, toward the kitchen, you passed by wall lockers and a door to the shop with that great Rudd cast iron instantaneous water heater.

What amazed me the most in this room was the gas-fired water heater and the storage of flammable liquids such as paint and thinners nearby on the bench. *Only in a fire station.* I remember Al at the bench nightly presiding over his fishing flies as the captain teased him unmercifully. Al was easy.

On the right side of the hall, front to rear, was the dayroom with a Gamewell Alarm System, maps, watchman bed, and the obligatory oak table and captain's chairs, the officer's dorm, locker room, and main dorm. The main dorm had three doors, one from the lockers and two from the hall. In 1968, we still used the Gamewell Alarm System. The alarm was a tap and bell system that would punch a number location onto a paper tape while, at the same time, sounding bells in the station. For example, if Box 3231 (at the corner of High Street and Thompson Avenue) was pulled, the station lights would all turn on at once and the bells would ring, four rounds as the tape would be punched with holes 3-2-3-1, four times. In the station was a card file that would show the address of the box. The officers were responsible to read and respond if appropriate.

Every night the bells were wound at 8:30 radio check. As a rookie, I got to sleep right under the dorm bell… a heart attack just waiting to happen. On the first strike of the bell, all the lights in the station

78

would drop (come on) and I would levitate about a foot off the bed. It was great fun for the old timers to watch a new guy freak out. Again, I was amazed that, if the alarm was not for us, the "FOGs" (F*# Old Guys) would resume snoring immediately, and I would lay in the darkness, heart pounding, with nowhere to go.

I was told by my Uncle Pat, who had worked with horses in the early days of the Richmond, California Department (where Granddad retired as chief in 1917) how the horses could tell, by the first round of bells, if the alarm was in their response district. If so, they would move out of their stalls and under the harnesses, prancing and snorting as if to say, "Get this harness on and let's go!" Behind Station Two was a garage that housed a 1958 GMC Civil Defense engine; at that stage we had some volunteers that would use the rig for training weekly. I was a member for a very short time in the early 60's. Now we have a state of the art workout room in its place.

The best place to be at night was in the apparatus room. There were two 60 watt globes that stayed on all night. In that glow, the red paint and gold leaf were breathtaking. I used to love to remove myself from the confusion of television, with the guys laughing and talking, to go sit behind the wheel of my rig. It was so quiet in comparison. The apparatus room had a life of its own, with unexplainable clicks and thumps, constant mechanical sounds only

1963 American-La France

heard in the quiet stillness of the night.

It continues to amaze me that this quiet could be so abruptly and forcefully broken by bells ringing, with engines starting, and eight men dressing as they

79

ran to the fire rigs shouting, "What's the address? What's burning?" Then to be standing on the tailboard of a 1963 American LaFrance open cab, as the engine pulled out and leaned into the turn, your buddy and one of your arms the only thing holding you as you finished buckling your turnout coat.

My mind began playing tricks on me. Suddenly I'm living back in the 1890's, as if I'm playing a part, and trying to envision what my uncle had told me about responding on the tailboard of a horse-drawn steamer. In the night, hearing the horses snorting, harnesses being buckled, and hooves prancing in anticipation as we/they climb aboard. I swear I can see one of the wild-eyed horses looking back at me as if to say, "What are you waiting for?" And with the crack of a whip, we're off! Out of the barn holding onto the bar, the smell of wood and coal burning, smoke exploding from the top of the steamer, kind of like a volcano. The sound of the steel clad hooves on cobblestones, sparks cascading over the

pavement then, leaning into the turn, the horses pull for all their worth, muscles straining as the steamer wheels slide back in line behind the steeds.

Snapping back to reality, I have now stepped into this line of glorious history. Looking ahead ten blocks, over the hose bed, past the driver and officer, through the open-cabbed windshield, the night sky was lit up, the glow of the fire reflecting off the low hanging clouds. It was a light show! On arrival we hit the ground running. Everyone knew what to do. Whether first in or last on the scene, the many hours of training paid off, and instinct took over. With the adrenalin pumping, my strength had doubled. It seemed I could lift anything. I could clear a six-foot fence, kick down a door, and was pushed beyond the limits of my courage by my brave buddies as we crawled into uncharted territory.

Chief, There's Fire in the Center Wall!

First Methodist Church Fire - Corner of Santa Clara and Eighth Streets

A full response for Engine Two, Truck Two, Engine Three, and Engine Five. Engine Two took the corner hydrant, and the crew entered the basement on the Eighth Street side. The report from Engine Two was a live line attack on the fire, assisted by Engine Five. Captain Steckler had me pull a 1-½ inch line to the west side of the structure. As I took my position, no one could see me in the smoke. I heard a crash, and looked up to see the explosion of a two foot diameter stained glass window, as Moe's helmeted head appeared, gasping for air. The thought went through my mind, *"Here's Moe!"* reminding me of the intro to the Johnny Carson Show. When he entered the tower, it was clear of smoke, but that changed quickly and bit him. The assistant chief called for a second alarm, Engine One and Truck One. Engine Two's officer, Burney Brooks, reported that the fire in the basement was under control.

The chief ordered me to check the main sanctuary. It was very dark as I made my way between two pews about a third of the way back. My foot slipped off the edge of a four foot hole. I caught myself on the pews to stop the fall. I'd better report my finding to the chief. As I turned back toward the center wall, I saw light all along the baseboard. There was fire in the walls! It was an old building and the "balloon construction" walls created a chimney from basement to attic. I should have shoved the nozzle through the plaster and fogged the hollows but I had been warned very sternly by the chief, whose religious belief had clouded his better judgment not to do any damage to this sacred place. No damage? Two hours later we could walk on the roof from the first floor.

When I reported my findings to the chief, he looked at me with glazed eyes and said, "Take the pickup to Station One and refill the Scott air tanks."

This is not what I wanted to do with so much action taking place. As I loaded the truck to go, I said to Jack, "I've got to fill the tanks and there's fire in the walls. The chief isn't doing anything; I don't think he believes me."

He smiled knowingly and gestured toward the eaves, which where belching black smoke, a telltale sign of more fire somewhere in the structure.

Jack said, "It's not over by a long shot! Those three guys better get off the roof and you'd better do what you're told."

In record time, I was back from Station One to find fire blowing out the roof. Now it's surround and drown. I found the line that I had laid in the smoke earlier, climbed the fire escape to the second floor, and shoved the nozzle through a 12 foot stained glass window. By now Truck One had taken the front and Ed was raising the ladder pipe into position. As I heard a rumble and ducked behind the wall next to the sanctuary window, flames blew out 30 feet and the roof dropped to the second floor. At the same time Pete, on the top of Truck Two, was engulfed in flames and smoke. Otis, observing from Engine Five, thought he was seeing the death of Pete. Jack tried to retract the ladder but Pete's axe handle was stuck between the rungs. With quick thinking, Jack extended the ladder and then tried again; it worked, and Pete came out steaming but unscathed, counting his body parts to be sure everything was there.

I was still in the same position but was now looking down at the roof that had once been 25 feet above me. One thousand gallons of

 water per minute from Truck One ladder pipe was now a waterfall dumping directly on top of me, and I was trying to climb under the brim of my helmet to catch a breath. **I was drowning in an inferno!** Eight hours later, we saved the foundation. *You win some, and you lose some.*

Don't Step on the Siren
(Do You Want Us to Die?)

Old Station One on Webb Avenue was built before motorized apparatus. As time went on, the horses were retired, and equipment grew in size until the rigs seemingly had to be pressure injected into their stalls. If you inhaled pulling out, you could scrape both sides of the door jamb at the same time… too little space, too many pieces of equipment.

There were three apparatus room doors with four rigs, two in front and two behind. The left door was just right for horse-drawn rigs but too narrow for the chief's car and the resuscitator wagon, so they were stacked in, one behind the other. If a medical call came in, someone would have to move the chief's car to let the resuscitator out. Well it worked in theory except, in those days, money was tight and the chief's battery needed replacing. We often had to push it out of the way to release the resuscitator.

The resuscitator wagon was a stock six-cylinder, 1950's vintage Ford station wagon. After attaching the red lights on the roof, two-way radio, and a giant siren on the front fender, the alternator was taxed beyond its capabilities. It was a real challenge to be driving at night, with red lights and headlights drawing so much current that, when the officer turned on the siren, the headlights would dim and the engine would start to die. If the siren was released, the lights would return, and the engine would cough to life again, sputtering into the darkness.

It was hilarious to watch. A call came in, one of the firefighters jumped into the chief's car and hit the starter, usually with no response.

A yell, "Hey guys! Help me push the chief's car!"

As it rolled into the street, the resuscitator would pull out. Halfway down the block approaching Park Street, you heard the siren wind up, saw the lights dim and the tail lights go out. The engine would buck, cough, and start to die.

The driver hollers, "Get off the siren!"

The officer screams back, "Do you want us killed?"

The driver shouts, "Do you want me to push the D*# thing?"

As the pedestrians watched in amazement and thought, *there go our professionals,* or asked "Is that Charlie Chaplin and friends?" they disappeared into the night. This could all be fixed but no one seemed to want to solve the problem. Pennies were pinched so badly in those days, you could be sent to the hardware store for six nails to fix the back fence. Yes, it really did run that way for a season. Happily, things have changed for the better with new equipment and better training. The down side is, I have less to write about, but real life was more entertaining than fiction.

What's "Psycho" Doing in Alameda?

House Fire, 1984 - Engine One is First to Arrive, 9:00 a.m.

We found another three-story Craftsman-style home with smoke coming from the eaves. The house was a little like the one in the movie "Psycho." Looking up from the tailboard of our rig, I could see the third floor widows. The curtains and shades were in tatters. They didn't match the outside, which was clean and orderly.

The captain said, "Let's go up the front stairs while Engine Three's crew goes to the basement."

I Could Have Died A Thousand Deaths

We donned our breathing apparatus and entered the main floor, going through the front door into the parlor, which was full of smoke but no fire. The three of us made a quick search; finding no people or fire, we saw a large staircase with a banister (envision "Gone with the Wind") leading to the third floor. At the top of the stairs, we were in a narrow hallway that extended front to rear. In the dark, narrow, smoke-filled hall, as our eyes adjusted, I realized the right wall was lined with furniture. I was thinking, *we must be on the right side of the house.* Moving down the hall, we saw doors to the left, a bathroom, bedroom, and utility room.

Having cleared those rooms, we joined up in the center of the hallway again. I saw light under one of the chest of drawers. Dropping down for a look in the smoke, there was a door visible behind the chest. We must have been in the center of the building, and there were rooms on the right side as well. Why the doors were blocked was beyond me. At this point in the almost total darkness, with breathing masks on, and our flashlight as the only source of illumination, we missed the door at the far end of the hall leading to this side of the building and a separate apartment. Pulling the furniture out, we tried to push the door open. It moved about two inches but something was stopping it from opening. *Could it be a body?* The captain shouted, "Get in there!" so Bob and I shoved with our shoulders. It moved another ten inches. I dropped down on my knees again to see, and slid through the door.

At first my mind was playing tricks as I felt something soft, maybe a body, but my flashlight helped me to see that it was only bags of clothing. With an adrenaline-filled push, the bundles moved away into a larger room and I stood up to find myself in a closet full of mothball-smelling, dusty, 1930's type dresses, and face to face with a fox coat, head still attached. A gasp and then the realization, *it's dead.* As I stood up, pushing aside the dresses, I used my light to look around the room and I was feeling like I wanted to back out, but George was pushing Bob, who was pushing me.

I saw before me the pile of clothing, a double bed with dirty yellow sheets, a shade-covered window with the tattered curtains, and newspapers scattered all over the floor. My light focused on the far end of the room with a bookshelf. Moving the light up the wall, it came to rest on two large, glowing yellow eyes, and I swore I heard the sound track of the shower scene from "Psycho." Bob had pushed into the room and there was no turning back now. George entered and I relaxed a bit as nothing was attacking me. I moved my light back to those eyes and realized that it was a stuffed owl. The head had rotted off and fallen down on the shelf upside down next to its body. There was an audible, "Whooo," as the three of us started to move through the apartment.

Leaving the bedroom, we entered a narrow kitchen, shades drawn, newspaper neatly covering the floor, sink full of dishes and appliances encrusted with grease. With every step, it felt more eerie, like something or someone I didn't want to encounter could be around the next corner. Entering the front room, still in darkness, were those tattered shades I saw from the street. The walls were lined with shelves full of hard-bound books and two old, dusty, overstuffed chairs.

Bob yelled, "No one's in the bathroom, no sign of fire. Let's get out of here!"

We tried the front door and realized that it was padlocked from the outside. We went back through the apartment, into the closet, said goodbye to the owl, and stepped out into the main hallway with a sigh of relief.

Report from Engine Three: "The fire was in the basement and it's under control." Now, with the smoke dissipating, we looked at the apartment door and saw the padlock. *Sure would have been easier to enter there.*

Captain George was now talking to another tenant who said, "I have lived here for five years and have never seen the upstairs tenant. Apparently he works nights, pays the rent by mail, and is heard but never seen."

I didn't know when I signed up for the fire department I would be an actor in scary movies, but even stranger things have happened.

Thank You, Binks

Bill Anderson was his name. Most people called him Binks. Who was he? The best friend we firefighters ever had. Most guys in later years didn't know what he had done for us. He should have been honored at our awards banquets every year. In later years he was thought somewhat of a joke by the guys that didn't know his history. When he would drop by for a visit or show up at an emergency, they would question why he was there. I have a scrapbook full of front page fire pictures and wonderfully written articles from the *Times-Star*, all because of this man. My biggest regret is that I didn't intervene on his behalf and honor him. A little late now, but he should be remembered...

I met Bill in the mid-1940's. He hung out at Webb Avenue, old Station One. Yes, he knew the time honored secrets of the "lean" in the oak chairs. He was accepted in the early days and helped in training evolution. Bill knew the rigs as well as anyone. When shorthanded at fires, he would do crowd control, set flares and pull hose the right way. He was appreciated and accepted by all for his help and knowledge of fire tactics. Bill, Dad and a handful of others had tried out for the department about the same time. Dad made it, but Bill couldn't pass the physical. He never got over the disappointment. But, instead of walking away, he became a volunteer.

As far back as I can remember, he lived across the street from Webb Avenue (old Station One) so that he could be near his friends and hear the fire alarms. Bill never married, but he had friends all over the city. Most mornings you could find him at Ole's Waffle Shop or see him walking down Park Street. He had his own business repairing all kinds of electronics including Game-well Alarm Systems, televisions, and ham radio equipment. Of course he had CB radios in the shop, at his house, and in his truck, all tuned to the fire channel.

Because he was always out and about in the city, he often beat the fire department on scene. That was no problem in the early years because everyone knew him and his story. Later, rumors started to the effect that he might be lighting fires because he was always there. This was far from the truth. He just loved being in and around the action. I'm much the same; we were kindred spirits though I got the job and could work legally. After joining the department, it was great to see Binks come for a visit or show up at a fire, but he was slowly falling out of favor due to the change of locations of Station One. We were now in a new building at Encinal and Park with not much time to sit around anymore. He did stay loyal to us and took pictures for close to 40 years.

A few years before his death, he moved to the city of San Leandro; somehow that seemed wrong, a loss to our community. We stopped seeing him. Part of what made Alameda, Alameda were its characters. He definitely was a character, a man of character. He died pretty much alone, not ever knowing that he will always be remembered, at least as long as I'm alive. Thank you, Bill Binks Anderson, the quiet hero of the AFD.

It's More like a Sepulcher than a Place of Laughter

Station Three, Built in 1923 - Grand Street and Pacific Avenue

The station is positioned on a corner in the center of town. I liked responding from this station; we would cover both ends of the city and didn't need to ride an ambulance.

There are two single apparatus rooms; one faces Pacific and the other faces Grand. A long path cuts through the grass to a brick porch with two steps up, under a metal awning to the heavy oak door. In 1949 Alameda celebrated its Centennial. Not to be outdone by the other stations, Station Three's crews tore down the back fence and used the old wood to make a saloon facade. The men of Alameda were told not to shave under penalty of arrest and incarceration during the days of this celebration. Clean-shaven men were put in the hoosegow (a trailer with bars surrounding) on Park Street and Santa Clara Avenue. Great fun.

1949 Centennial
Station 3

Joe

Jack

Jack

Al

Dad

Al

Red

Red Dog Saloon

I started negotiating Station Three's steps at about age three, when Mom and I would visit Dad. The station has windows on either side of the front door; the sign above makes it clear that you have arrived at Station Three of the Alameda Fire Department. The left (or Pacific) wing contains a hall with lockers and the main dorm extending to Engine Four's apparatus bay. To the right wing was the office, officer's dorm, and Engine Three's apparatus bay. Behind Engine Three was a small workout room and shop. There's

nothing better for the lungs than to be riding the Aerodyne exercise bicycle when Engine Three started... choke, cough! On the inside wall was a storage room, bathroom and turnout/phone room.

I Could Have Died A Thousand Deaths

Twelve years after my retirement, upon entering the front door of this station built in 1923, all of my senses are assaulted anew as the memories flooded in. But in 2006, the building was condemned. The living area sits empty and the feel is more like a sepulcher (tomb) then a place of laughter and music. The sounds of the auxiliary generator being run and chain saws being tested are gone. Shadows invade all areas; the cold and slightly musty smell cannot eliminate the warmth in my heart for this amazing building. There are great memories of the years of service to its community, with the guys sitting on the front porch on Sunday afternoons in the fall talking to kids as they walked by, or waxing the engine as we waited for the next, inevitable emergency. We even had time in those days to whiten the Goodyear lettering on the tires. It was a pleasure to see my family arrive for a visit, as Mom and I had done so many years before. This was good stuff!

Some things need to be saved; new is not always better. The floors in the station are not waxed anymore, but strewn with all kinds of debris. The kitchen where we cooked 100 tons of popcorn is now in need of "Tim, the Tool Man, Taylor." Only the apparatus rooms are being used. Life has moved next door to a Victorian. As I walk through this wonderful structure, I feel as though I'm attending a wake at the home I lived in for 13 years. After all these years in and around this sanctuary, the smell has changed. The feeling has gone from warmth to cold, from light to dark, from laughter to silence, from clean and waxed to debris-strewn and dusty. Now the odor of dry rot has replaced the aroma of life. The district map that Ed and I colored so many years ago still hangs in the hallway. I look quickly to see if my secret is still on the map, and it is. Some traditions are still here. Good bye, old friend!

The Map

Ed and I were ordered by the chief to color a new city map designating, First In (still, or single unit response) Districts. We worked hard for a couple of weeks in between runs, rig and station maintenance, inspections, and bicycle licensing, with the chief

checking every shift to see what was holding us up. The day came when the job was finished and finally the chief was happy. But something was missing. I decided it was my map. What could I do to mark it (kind of like a male dog marking his territory)? I know... I'll draw a man swimming for his life from a great white shark in one of the Harbor Bay lagoons. Then I'll post an ever-so-small sign that says, "No Swimming." Now that felt good. I don't think anyone ever noticed but, every time I went to the map, I knew.

Now You Know I'm Whacky!

Station Three, One Summer Afternoon in 1981, About 5:00

I entered the dorm to make up my bed. Mike was fairly new in the department; even then it was a pleasure to work with him. Anyway, as the story goes, I was making my bed and Mike came in to make his. We were passing the time of day when I looked down at my blanket and something dawned on me. I started laughing. Mike asked, "What's so funny?"

93

I Could Have Died A Thousand Deaths

I said, "Ya know, it's been 13 years and I just realized I've never washed my blankets."

He looked at me with suspicion. Now his opinion of me has been confirmed... I'm nuts. He laughed, then I also laughed in disbelief that so much time has escaped me.

The story continues: The year is now 1993. I am lieutenant at Station Three. Tonight, well-decorated Captain Mike D'Orazi is working a trade. The time is about 5:00 p.m. and I am making my bed, which is currently in the officer's dorm. In walks Mike to make his bed. I look down at my same blankets and, déjà vu, I start to laugh. Mike again asks, "What's so funny?"

I reply, "Ya know, Mike, it just dawned on me that it's been 25 years and I still haven't washed my blankets!"

Now it's confirmed what he thought for a long time. I really am whacky. So tradition dictated that I never laundered my blankets until after my retirement. However, I do want everyone to know that my sheets were changed and I showered on a regular basis.

In 2015, that great blanket is still with me, a reminder of hundreds of nights of being thrown back reluctantly as another call came in and I had to leave the warmth of my wonderful, odiferous cover.

Who Needs an Engine to Put Out a Fire?
Station Three, 1970, 7:00 p.m.

I was standing watch in the front room when the doorbell rang. A woman pleaded frantically, "My kitchen stove is on fire, next door!"

I yelled down the hall, "Captain Steckler, Captain Dockery, there's a stove fire next door!"

I entered Engine Three's apparatus room and opened the overhead door. The woman was now on the lawn screaming. I grabbed the CO2 extinguisher from Engine Three and reasoned to myself, *I'll just run next door and put it out. No sweat, what could go wrong?*

Problem 1 – I was the firefighter on Engine Five and should have stayed with that crew.

Problem 2 - I presumed, *it's no big deal and I'll have it out before either rig is started.*

Problem 3 - I met the woman next door and said, "Which house?"

She screamed, "Follow me!"

Problem 4 - Three houses down the street, I stopped her and asked again, "Which house?"

She pointed another half-block away, across the intersection. I saw flames through the second story window. *I've screwed up big time,* I realized. No one knew where I was, Captain Dockery couldn't leave without me, so he and the driver were frantically combing the station; I was missing in action.

I heard Engine Three starting. It was as far back to Station Three as to the house so I figured I might as well be fired for trying to extinguish the blaze instead of for running from it. By the time I had covered ¾ of a block with the thirty pounds of extinguisher on my shoulder, I was getting winded and had a long flight of stairs, which I took two at a time, to the second floor. Standing at the door, I realized I didn't even have my turnout coat or helmet. I concluded, *Oh well, maybe if I burn up I won't get in trouble.* On

I Could Have Died A Thousand Deaths

entering the house, I made my way to the kitchen and saw flames extending from the stovetop to the ceiling.

As I extinguished the fire, I heard Engine Three's radio outside, "6-3 to Central, 6-3's on the scene. We will be pulling the live line."

Through the front window I could see the guys pulling the live line and coming up the stairs. I arrived at the door from the inside at the same moment Captain Steckler arrived.

I opened the door for him and said, "The fire is out."

The look on his face spoke volumes: *How'd you do that? You're on the engine behind us!* Engine Five had finally given up looking for me and was now on the scene. Captain Dockery, on seeing me, would have used an axe between my eyes, if he had one, to show his relief. I said nothing more, but knew that my life was in jeopardy when we returned to the station. There was no way to explain what I was thinking.

Captain Dockery, with the patience of a saint, chewed my butt and asked about my reasoning, inquired about my I.Q., finally took pity on me, and kept my faux pas from the chief. Needless to say, that mistake was never repeated. To my knowledge, I'm the only firefighter on two legs to be first in to the scene of a fire, extinguish it single handedly and not have to write the report.

Five Hundred Cubic Feet of Trouble

Station Four, Fountain and Jackson - Built in 1923

The station was situated on the east end of town. Built in 1923, a one-story rectangle with windows covered by Venetian blinds all the way around. On entering the front door, you passed through an anteroom and counter to the hallway, and then left to the dayroom. In the center of the dayroom was an oak table and captain's chairs, in the corner a television, and on the west wall a Gamewell Alarm System. To the south were the officer's dorm and office. Leaving the dayroom, looking west down the hall on the right, was the anteroom, kitchen and bathroom. This bathroom was more like the type used in a city office building than the other stations, with small white tiles on the floor and lower walls, stand-alone sinks and built-in urinals that stood shoulder high and descended into the floor. At the end of the hall was the door to the apparatus room. On the left side of the hall were the city and hydrant maps. Two-thirds of the way down, turn left to a locker hall, and then left again into the main dorm.

I can still hear Russ snoring so loud it did me no good to try to sleep. Russ was a great guy; he was my next-door neighbor on Beach Road. He and his wife, Vivian, looked after my brother and me when Dad died. It was truly an honor to get to work with him, even though he had the bad habit of growing horseradish and bringing it to the station to be ground up. Russ was banned to the backyard when grinding. He would come in, eyes swollen and nose running, but smiling, a glutton for punishment. Russ also had the reputation for wearing out shovels; he's the only man I've ever heard of that dug his own swimming pool by hand.

At the far left end of the main hall was a small shop. Prominent in the corner was a great Rudd cast iron instantaneous water heater that had to be as old as the station. In that room, if you stood very still, you could feel the ghost of Al at the bench tying fishing flies. The building was pretty basic compared to the others. The one most interesting bit of trivia had to do with its apparatus room. The apparatus room doors, again, were arched wood with window panels. The rig was a 1950's vintage American LaFrance, 1250 gallon-a-minute pumper that barely fit through the doors.

On the floor, you could see an outline in the concrete that looked like a pit that had been paved over. I inquired of this and was told, due to safety issues and lack of use, the pit had been filled in by the city. This made good sense, though the way it had been done was a curiosity. It seemed that, rather than backfill with dirt and then slab over with four or five inches of concrete, Chief Servente had an in with Rhodes and Jamison Ready-Mix Company, so they filled the whole pit with leftover concrete. That means that someday in the far distant future, when contractors are tearing down the station to put in a shopping center or an apartment building, they will scratch their heads on finding a block of concrete 4 x 5 x 25 feet, or five hundred cubic feet of trouble. And wonder, *"Why?"*

*The screams were long silent now as we
continued our battle. No other tactic at
this point, except to surround and drown.*

What's the Address? Go Outside and Look!

Tahoe Apartments Fire - 1824 Central Avenue
Wednesday, February 7, 1973, 8:13 p.m.

I was at home on Marina Drive on the living room floor playing
with my family and watching television. For some reason, though I
don't remember why, my wife said that we looked at each other as
if we heard an unusual sound and, within five minutes, a call came
in from Central Fire. Dispatch was recalling me to work, "The
middle of town is burning."

"What's the address?" I asked.

"Go outside and look; you'll see where to go."

I didn't know at the time, but I soon would. A jet fighter had fallen
from 30,000 feet. Dispatch was right. As I looked from my front
door about three miles west, the whole sky was lit up. Driving
down Lincoln, I couldn't get past Oak Street because of the traffic
already out to see this extravaganza. I turned west on Pacific and
was able to get to Lafayette, where I left my car and hoofed it to
the scene. At the time I didn't know what had happened except that
a four-story apartment building was fully involved, with a Victorian to the east and two apartment buildings to the south and west
starting to burn.

Approaching the front, Engine One was set up with a long lay, 2-½
inch supply line, not nearly enough water to equip the three hoses
going to Truck 1 with three hand-held lines. Engine One was at the

point of pulling a vacuum on the main hydrant and needed another supply. It was about as effective as a fire extinguisher.

Tahoe Apartments

Truck One was setting up as a water tower but only had one 2-½ inch supply. The radios in the background were screaming for water. All of our rigs were committed around the perimeter, as the call had gone out for mutual aid. I told Marv that I would get him another supply. Reporting to the chief, he told me to grab any incoming mutual aid engine and to lay a line across town. I flagged an Oakland hose wagon and we laid cross town to Lincoln Avenue on another water grid. At the time, Oakland had three-inch hose and we had 2-½ inch. These were incompatible and Oakland didn't carry adapters. As we emptied the last of the hose at the hydrant, a Coast Guard rig was passing by. They had adapters and were able to hook up and pump to Engine One.

Naval Air Station crash trucks had arrived and were setting up foam. From there, I went to help the captain setting up 2-½ inch hose lines and quick-training volunteers to hold them. I drug a supply line from another engine to the corner of Central and Union. As I was hooking up, the northeast corner of the building collapsed. I could feel the intense heat washing over me. I wanted to run but adrenalin helped me fight the heat as I succeeded in turning on the water. My pants were steaming as I ran for shelter a half-block away. Looking back, most of the block was on fire. People had come out of the woodwork and firefighters were assigning civilians to hold nozzles so that they could put more lines into play. Traffic was hindering the movement of apparatus. It was orchestrated chaos. The screams were long silent now as we continued our battle. No other tactic at this point, except to surround and drown.

3:00 a.m. - The building had collapsed in on itself. Smoke and steam were rising hundreds of feet into the air. In the floodlights what was left of the four-story building was now reduced to 12 feet of collapsed stucco and rebar. Most of the wood had been consumed. I found myself sitting on a pile of stucco hidden in the steam with my 2-½ inch hose flooding the hot spots below. The thought came to mind that, *somewhere below are people, people that just six hours earlier were living life as usual. But suddenly they're gone.* I hoped they had made peace with God (Romans 10:9, 10).

A week later, we were still there investigating, excavating and wondering why. It took a crane digging below ground level to find signs of the plane. Its engine had gone through a four-story building, a concrete slab, and 15 feet into the earth. The only remains found of the pilot were some wrist bone and the cuff of his flight jacket. There was very little sign of the eleven people

I Could Have Died A Thousand Deaths

Morning After

unaccounted for. Four months after the fire, we were still being greeted by people on the street, with thanks. They made us feel like heroes.

"Attention all Stations! There has been an airplane crash in the vicinity of Encinal & Grand Street. All companies respond."

Another Perspective on the Tahoe Apartments Fire

Firefighter Bud Steers' Account as Engineer on Engine Two

Recollections of my Engine Two operations, responding to and at the fiery site of the Navy jet crash into the Tahoe Apartments in Alameda, California. There are numerous articles about this spectacular and tragic event, and I suggest that they be read in conjunction with my account.

SUCH AS:

It was a Navy A-7-E Corsair from Lemoore Naval Air Station,

piloted by Lieutenant Robert Lee Ward, an experienced, college educated, and former instructor pilot.

It seems that the plane dove from 30,000 feet at a very steep angle and crashed at speed nearing Mach-1. These are some of my recollections as follows:

I was on duty at Alameda Fire Department Station Two, seated in the office at the front of the building and across the hall from the large main operations room. It was after the evening meal at about 8:00 p.m. and time for study or other personal things. I read the daily fire log for 7 February 1973, which is a normal and usual thing, when I heard a loud screeching sound followed by a boom and a shaking/shudder, like a mild earthquake. I had no idea what had happened, but I knew it was something big that would probably need a response by Engine Two. I opened the door on the other side of the office leading to the apparatus room, hit the door-open button, put on my turnout jacket and, with helmet in hand, I mounted Engine Two and started the engine.

Somewhere in this process I heard the report from Central, **"Attention all stations! There has been an airplane crash in the vicinity of Encinal & Grand. All companies respond."**

This was a very unusual and seldom heard dispatch from Central. I am ready to go and with the echo of the strange dispatch in my ears, Lieutenant Kennon swung into his seat saying, "Let's roll!"

Pulling out through the apparatus door, as we departed we could see the fire reaching high into the sky probably 100 feet or more. We chose to take Central Avenue which put us exactly in front of the Tahoe Apartments. Engine One was already on scene and had "laid in" (a fire department term for hose evolution). It looked like a war zone with glass and debris everywhere, and the building totally involved, power & phone lines drooping to the sidewalk. Crowds of very excited citizens had come to observe this spectacular happening. We had planned to "lay out" to the next hydrant but, when Lieutenant Kennon made his first pull of hose off the tailboard, the anxious citizens pulled all 2,000 feet of our 2-1/2 inch hose onto the ground in what looked like one giant mass of spaghetti.

During the initial happenings, I noticed a husky young man with a very popular, appropriately labeled, SUPERMAN T-shirt climb a rain downspout pipe and rescue a young woman and her small dog from the first floor window on the west side. With all our 2-1/2 inch hose laying in a pile on the street, I told Lieutenant Kennon that I was going to find a hydrant and he said okay. So I ended up one street south on Alameda Avenue. I had found a wonderful high-volume, green top hydrant on the back side of the fire scene and adjacent to an alley that had some sort of access to the apartments.

I busied myself hooking up the steamer (large diameter hose) to the hydrant and had no more then gotten that done, when a young man excitedly came to me saying, "I am a Redding volunteer fireman. How can I help?"

I asked him to go to Central Avenue on the other side of the fire and gather up as much 2-1/2 inch hose with a yellow I.D. band around the fittings. It was just a short while later that he returned with two or three other young men and all my hose loaded on the hood and roof of his Rambler American.

This Redding volunteer fireman, with aid from his recruited friends, hooked together three 2-1/2 inch lines to reach the fire and, with instructions from me, attached nozzles. I have no way of knowing who manned those lines. My crew then laid hose bundles and a live line to the fire scene and, of course, I am busy with instructing my crew and happily charging each line. I still have two outlets unused when I see an Oakland fire engine laying two of their 2-3/4 inch lines toward me down the alley. With crowds of animated citizens looking on, Hallelujah, I have two Oakland adaptors and attach and charge those lines also. I can only suppose that they were fitted with Oakland fire department nozzles. I would really love to have a photo of Engine Two in this pumping condition. All the many hours of training did pay off as our team held together in a time of great crisis.

Adrenaline

Adrenalin is the most descriptive word I can think of to explain this job. At 7:15 a.m., I hug my wife and kids and jump on my bike for a leisurely ride to the station. No matter what the previous shift had been like, there were at least 24 hours of rest to unwind. The next morning, though, I would be happy to return to work and see the guys. You could quickly tell, by the tenor of the greeting and the facial expressions of the off-going crew, what their night had been like. I always looked for the old timers. They didn't move stations much, the advantage of seniority. There was always an unexpected face, a newer guy who had been reassigned from his regular station for sick or vacation coverage. The city of Alameda was only 2 by 5 miles in size with four stations. You could sometimes go a year and miss seeing friends you had worked with in the past. I stayed pretty much with my regular crew, while others made numerous trades for personal reasons. With different people, the dynamics of the crew were always different. That's why training was so important. Repetition works.

I Could Have Died A Thousand Deaths

In 1968, we had to live within 40 miles of the city limits. Laura and I chose Alameda, but most guys moved over the hill to Livermore or Pleasanton as you got more house for the money, but also more commute time. I loved living in the city; I often knew the house and the people we were helping. My family would bike to the station after school or on Sunday afternoon for a visit. The crews were always happy to see them; it made my day easier knowing the girls were within a couple of miles of the station. In case of an emergency, I could get home. On inspection near our house, we often detoured by to greet the kids and neighbors. It was a repeat of Dad's legacy; in the 1940's, Dad had done the same thing. I could hear the rig coming; that sound was so powerful. Looking up at the engine from the sidewalk, all four feet of me were in awe. The guys smiling down from this great red and gold machine seemed like super heroes. Opened cab, chain drive, loaded with hose and ladders, the picture is seared into my mind.

I did get to walk in my dad's footsteps, my destiny. It made more sense to me to be living and helping the community I was a part of. At home on my days off, the sound of sirens always piqued my interest. The amount and direction of those sirens converging told something about the nature of the call. If the rigs continued to roll through, it was probably a fire. If all but one siren stopped en route, it was probably a false alarm or an emergency medical call. Again, if all the rigs continued to the location, I would get in my car and go to the scene. Sometimes Erin and Bree would ride along to watch the excitement from our car. They still like to kid me about how scared they were, but they always wanted to ride along. What fun!

The Fire Bike

Orange County Choppers - Dedication for 9/11

I was watching a rerun of Orange County Choppers (OCC) on television yesterday. Their business is building custom motor-cycles. OCC had been commissioned to create a 9/11 Memorial Bike to be dedicated in the memory of 343 fallen firefighters who died in New York City on September 11, 2001. I remembered back to 9/11, watching on television as people fled to escape the falling buildings. Then, news cameras seemed to focus on firefighters moving in the opposite direction... toward the towers. They came from all over to fight this fatal battle. I am a fourth generation firefighter with a career of 25 years under my belt. I could tell by their faces that they were nervous about going into the biggest holocaust in U.S. history. That was their job. So this band of brothers, who had trained together, lived and ate together, had one purpose, to defeat the enemy and protect the innocent. So, bravely, they entered hell undaunted. The men fought valiantly against this raging foe, this evil emissary of death and destruction perpetrated in the name of a god that is counterfeit but has beguiled 1,500,000,000 people. These men are true heroes, every one of them.

OCC had chosen to say thank you in iron and gold leaf, a memorial that will remind us of 9/11. During the two hours of creation, fabrication, welding, grinding, yelling, frustration, and plan changes, we saw a marvel become reality. Now the time had arrived to *fire it up*. Every man at OCC was gathered around, as was I, to see and hear this wonderful creation come to life. Now the team was of one accord and one purpose, to complete the task. I could see this was a special bike. The men's faces were taut, eyes focused, ears ready, with a few tears of emotion from otherwise stoic expressions. Vince had the honor of pressing the starter button as the once silent bike roared to life. The sound was strong,

testosterone-filled power at ignition, an explosion of emotion, a release of controlled violence... music to my ears.

This music takes me back in time, three years into my fire career and the starter button of a Seagrave 100 foot aerial ladder truck, powered by a V8, 1971 Detroit diesel, with a 6-speed Alison transmission. I was in the driver's seat of the biggest and best aerial ladder truck in our department. This machine, the Harley Davidson of the Alameda Fire Department (AFD), was mine to ride. When I heard the OCC Fire Bike start, it took me back to 1971, Station One at 3:00 a.m., in bed and hearing the alarm bells clang and the radio announcing,

"Attention all stations! We have the report of a three-story Victorian on fire at 1616 Grand Street. This will be a full response for Engine Three, Engine Five, Engine One, and Truck One."

"That's us! Let's go." All the guys were out of bed and into our boots, pants up and buckled in one motion. Ten seconds later, taking turns through the dorm room door and down the stairs two at a time, through the apparatus room door, into the garage which was still in darkness. Not a problem. I could find Truck One with my eyes closed. We moved through the shadows toward that wonderful red and gold leafed iron creation whose only purpose is to save lives. As I stepped up behind the wheel of Truck One, to my left Engine One started, expelling a great cloud of black diesel smoke (we have nicknamed Engine One "The Super Skunk" for that reason). With my right hand, I reached down to find the batteries disconnect, two turns in either direction, and the sound of the fuel pump began to cycle. With my left hand, I pressed the two starter buttons and the Detroit diesel growled, then roared to life. With one sweep of my right index finger across the rocker switches, the light bar was activated and the reflection in the side of Engine One caused a rush of adrenaline. I loved this testosterone-filled job!

Engine One pulled out ahead of us. I thought, *Come on, Cap! Let's go! No sweat... we've got the horse power. I'll catch up. The* captain stepped in and I released the air brakes. We rolled out across the driveway. I made a right turn and, as I straightened out, my throttle foot was to the floor. The diesel screamed to life. It's the only other sound I know of that comes close is the sound of that OCC Fire Bike. Thank you, Paul, Paul, Jr., Rick, Vince, and Jason. Did I say I loved this job? Eight blocks down Encinal, we caught up with Engine One. We saw black smoke exploding from its 864 cubic inch Mac-O-Dine turbo V8 every time he shifted. Four blocks ahead we saw the night sky lit up, clouds reflecting the fire as it broke through the roof.

Engine Three arrived and was on the radio. "Engine Three to

Central. We have a fully involved three-story Victorian. We're going through the front door. Engine Five, lay a supply line."

"Roger!"

"Truck One, we'll need the aerial ladder to the roof for ventilation and rescue."

"Roger. Will co," replied Truck One.

"Engine One, we'll need fire lines to the rear of the house."

"Roger!"

"Three Chief to Central, send a second alarm."

"Roger, Three Chief!"

Two hours later, testosterone depleted, adrenaline released, soaking wet, black from soot and smoke, the fire is out. We saved two but lost one, not good enough. No loss of life is acceptable. All this memory was triggered by the sound of that wonderful OCC machine. Speaking for the men I have associated with over the years: sounds, scents, and experiences are important to us. They bring us back in time to situations, good and bad, that make up who we are today.

Testosterone-filled experiences help us find our place in this world. Testosterone, that crazy hormone that makes men who we are, often gets a bad rap but, used for the right purpose, is extremely necessary. It can make heroes of regular guys; it enabled me to jump over a six foot fence in full fire gear, air tank on my back and a hose in my right hand; it protects families, and performs great feats of strength defending our country.

Used wrongly, it can cause fights, wars, gang violence, and a lifetime of pain. Testosterone controlled can best be described by a biblical verse, **Matthew 5:5**, *"Blessed are the meek for they will inherit the earth."* The word meek here in Greek is translated "harnessed strength," or testosterone reigned in. It's a picture of two plow horses or a team of fire horses linked together. Their combined strength is much more than what a single horse could do. I once demonstrated two D9 Caterpillar tractors welded side-by-side for strip mining. The combined power of the two under the control of one man was beyond belief. The machines could slice through solid granite.

This is what I have learned in my 74 years: A team pulling together can solve most problems. I learned that in organized sports, the Army and, again, I learned this truth in the fire department. On the other hand, a group of men pulling for themselves quickly causes destruction and chaos. We need to be team players in life. I think that is why, if boys aren't moved in a positive direction while they are still pliable, they will find a different team called the Crypts or the Bloods. From birth, parents need to understand that hormones are in motion. They need to be controlled, channeled, and directed. Another word for this is to be *discipled*. I-phones and I-pods cannot take the place of a man-to-boy or a man-to-man relationship.

Single mothers need to understand this and seek out strong role models for their sons. If discipled well, men save society, even give their lives if necessary for whomever they are called to help. If we're wrongly influenced, we can become pilots that fly into tall buildings. Discipline and being discipled is a natural life process that human nature would rather circumvent. But discipline works well. I had men, seasoned men, to test me. It was up to me to listen and learn. My time would come. It's called apprenticeship in the trades. We go through many seasons of growth: birth, infancy, adolescence, young adulthood and, hopefully, maturity and wisdom. **Proverbs 9:10**, *"The reverence of the Lord is the beginning of wisdom and the knowledge of the holy one is understanding."*

Thirty years old, ten years out of high school, ten years in the trades, I had driven most everything on the highway and in heavy construction. I had proven myself on all types of equipment, having risen from a steam cleaning rack at Peterson Tractor to head test pilot of all experimental equipment being built for Caterpillar. Then I chose to take a chance and started over. I followed my dad, granddad, uncle, father-in-law and great granddad into the fire department at age 27. I was going through the learning process all over again, with new mentors this time: my chief, captain, lieutenant and peers. None of the men seemed to care about my credentials. Their advice to me was to shut up, grab a broom and do what you're told. Time will sort things out.

July 31, 2011, 70 years old and starting over again. We had just left our church of ten years. We had left the security of Patty's salary and my reputation as a Bible and history teacher for a deeper walk with my ultimate mentor, the Lord God. **Psalm 119:105**, *"Your word is a lamp to my feet and a light to my path."* It's time once more to sit down, shut up, listen and start over again.

Returning to the chopper "build," it was time to present the Fire Bike to the FDNY. In front of a downtown station, surrounded by family and fire friends, OCC added a final touch to the Bike, a rivet found by one of the firefighters in the rubble of the Twin Towers. Paul, Jr. placed it on the tank and the tribute was complete. The look on the faces of all present was satisfaction of a job well done and recognition of 343 men that had left their families and friends for a higher calling. Their job was done but we must learn from their example and leave the world a better place than we found it. Thank you, men of Orange County Choppers.

A final word to every man reading this: think of the "build" in your own life. Think of your gifting and your own unique talents. They are to be used. God has made you this way; He has a plan for your life. Do you want Him or do you want the status quo? But, you say, "Life isn't fair! I didn't have a dad." Neither did I. You say, "I was poor!" So was I. You say, "My nationality hinders me." Oh, really? I am now the minority and was skipped over five times for the lieutenant's job in the AFD because of my affiliation with Christ. Get over it! We all have differences, but God is still God, the great equalizer. He has a unique plan for you and only you. It takes work, no excuses; it will hurt, it will cause frustration and pain, but it will also bring direction, hope, fulfillment, satisfaction and purpose. You can't get it from a book written about purpose. Real purpose comes from God. Your task is to find it. To younger men: if you need help, look for an older man that you respect and ask him for it, then listen. We older men have a lot to share. You only need to request it.

Barn Full of Great Steeds

(There's That Horse Manure Again)

Station One, January 1973, 10:00 p.m.

Four years had passed and I'm on duty at our "new" Station One at the corner of Encinal and Park Streets. Probation was completed. I had quite a few fires under my belt; I was beginning to feel that I was truly accepted and pretty comfortable in the fire department. The time was 2200 hours. I had just left Harry, Moe, Ed, and Otis in the dayroom to check out the rigs before bed. I was driving Truck One that night, a 1972 Seagrave 100 foot aerial, powered by

I Could Have Died A Thousand Deaths

an 8V71 Detroit Diesel, with a six-speed automatic Allison transmission. Since the day I first saw and heard it, I knew it was mine to tame. Coming from the lights of the dayroom into the dimness of the apparatus room, there was that smell I loved so much: diesel from the rigs and smoke emanating from a row of turnout coats and helmets.

I surveyed the equipment and was struck by the stillness in this barn full of great steeds calmly in their stalls, fully equipped and quiet.

Again, my mind is in the 1890's. I could feel a tension, I could hear the shake of a head and swish of the mane, I could see flesh on the horse's back ripple and hooves clicking on the pavement. There was a munching of hay, and a slight whinny of greeting as I drew

near. Their muscles were flexed yet tethered, waiting to be spurred into life. The satisfaction of knowing that I could control this power was thrilling. Now I think of the fragment of leather bridle I still have from the horse my great grandfather rode to many fires in his 30 years as chief in Grand Rapids, Michigan. His brother was a

114

captain; his son, my grandfather. Dad had told me their stories and of my grandfather who was also a chief in Richmond, California. Granddad's brother-in-law was a mechanic for Richmond and assembled their first aerial ladder truck.

Uncle Pat tells of his early years tending the fire horses, Jennie and Bessie. As I mentioned before, these horses would stand quietly in their open stalls until the alarm bells struck. With the first strike, the fillies would start to snort and prance; if the sequence of bells was right, they knew by the count, and would move out under the harnesses that hung from the apparatus room ceiling. The harnesses were pre-attached to the steamer. The teamster would lower the harnesses, cinch the buckles, and take his position at their reigns, with a look over his shoulder to see if the men were through stoking the burners and onboard. A quick nod from the captain and they were off. I wish I could have experienced that. The closest I'll ever be to them is in the dim light of this garage, standing in their footsteps, feeling their spirits.

The glow from the dispatch room and one 60-watt bulb on the opposite wall were the only source of illumination. Truck One (5-1) was to the far left at the front, Engine One (6-1) to its right, then came a 1960's vintage Ford station wagon (resuscitator car) and the chief's car. I walked to Truck One and mentally went through every cabinet to remind myself of the equipment stored within; then to Engine One, a 1968 Mack, 864 cubic inch twin turbo V8. From the driver's seat, I started my simulated check. Lights, pump, engagement lever, rev engine to see tachometer and speedometer move to be sure that the pump is engaged, and set the air brakes. As I moved from the cab to the pump panel, I always walked out away from the rig to look at the panel from a distance (perspective) to see and count every gate (valve), tank dump, live line gate, pressure relief, and gauges. Then, closing my eyes, I would touch every gate handle. Better to do this at 10:00 p.m. than to be fumbling for gate 3 or 5, and the live line at 3:00 in the morning, blurry eyed with people screaming, "Give me water!" *I must confess at this point that I am truly in love with these mechanical marvels.*

2:00 a.m. - I awoke to the Buck Horn and Driftwood bars across the street unloading their drunks. The gas station had cars coming and going, and every kid in Alameda was hanging out at Jack in the Box. Don't they know we need our sleep? Summertime is the worst; Station One is cinder block construction without air conditioning. We needed the windows open, but the noise was terrible. As I rested there trying to get back to sleep, my eyes surveyed the dark quiet of the dorm. Across the room I could see the glow of a cigarette as Ed took a few drags and returned to sleep. In another location I could see the glow of a cigarette sitting on its filter on the seat of a wooden chair burning itself out... could be Jack. *Only in a fire station,* I mused. Quite a few of the old timers did this. Often, when cleaning the dorm, we would find burned out cigarettes sitting upright on their filters or a scorch spot on the chair. Times truly have changed, **but I will always desire the ancient paths.**

Motorcycles - In the Living Room?

Station One, Mid-1970's, 1:00 a.m.

The crew was catching Z's. At this time we were dispatched from the main station. When a call came in, all stations heard the initial conversation. I awakened to the voice of Archie and the often-heard phrase, "Alameda Fire Department." The plea of a female voice on the other end was so alarming, "There's fire coming out the windows of a house across the street and people are trapped!"

Before the lights dropped (turned on) or we were dispatched, the beds were emptied and everyone was moving down the stairs and across the apparatus room to the rigs. I was driving Truck One. Otis was driving Engine One, "What's the address?"

"Otis Drive at Park Avenue."

With adrenalin pumping, I stepped up and slipped behind the wheel of the truck. "Hey, Otis, it's on Otis Drive!"

Otis already had the Mack started. With my right hand I turned the batteries, disconnected two clicks. With my left hand, I hit the two starter buttons and the Detroit diesel came to life. *What a sweet sound.* A sweep of my right fingers across the dash and all the lights were on. The dash panel has always looked great lit up, and the rotating beacons reflecting off the walls and other apparatus added more adrenalin to the mix. "Come on, lieutenant. Let's go!" Engine One is out the door and a half block away as we pull onto Encinal and left onto Park Street. *I'll catch them, no sweat.*

Dispatch is on the radio to Engine One: "We've received numerous calls. There seems to have been an explosion. People are trapped."

Engine One was accelerating through San Jose Avenue. The Mac-O-Dine diesel has always been set too fuel rich; we could tell when the engineer has his foot in it or was changing gears from the black smoke of the exhaust. Still, Truck One had pulled within 300 feet. As we neared the intersection of Park Street and Otis Drive, the engine was in the turn, and we could see the reflection of fire and light on its side. I looked as we came around the corner and saw people running frantically, silhouetted in the flames.

The call from the captain on Engine One: "A fully involved duplex. Engine One to Central, we'll be pulling the live line and going in the front door. Central to Engine Three, pull Engine One a supply line."

"Engine Three, Roger, will do."

Engine One was directly in front of the house. We staged across the street and a little forward as we didn't need the aerial. My crew has gone to rescue. Being a dry foot (driver), I stayed with the truck. No ladders were needed so I pulled a supply line from Engine One to the hydrant and turned on the water.

It's always a great feeling when the water fills the hose and the engineer, Otis, acknowledges with relief, "We have water!"

Engine Three had arrived; they were pulling more lines around the back. People on the sidewalk were screaming, "People are inside!"

All immediate tasks were covered. What could I do? I pulled another pre-connected line and shoved it in the front window as the fire was still resisting entry through the front of the building. The captain and Bob were finally making headway through the door but it was tough going. The fire was so hot and was beating them back. I thought to myself, *people are in there,* as I charged my line

and hit the fire, it blew back in my face, hot and wet. I ducked a little and kept my line in until Steck and Bob were inside.

Back to the truck for the generator because they needed lights. As I pulled the extension cord and flood lights through the door and illuminated the now darkened structure, the scene in the front room took me aback, soot-covered walls radiating heat, the odor of wet, charred wood, two over-stuffed chairs, a coffee table, a queen sized hide-a-bed opened out, and two motorcycles. Wait! Motorcycles? *What the hell are two motorcycles doing in the living room?*

The guys found Peggy behind a partially burned sliding door, right where my line had been trained. I didn't realize, when I stuffed the hose in the window, that I was protecting and cooling her with the water curtain. In the back bedroom, George found a naked teenage boy and was trying to carry him through the living room and out but he needed more help as the boy's skin was slippery and hard to hold onto; we were calf deep in water.

As I set the floodlights down, I received a severe shock. The extension cord had a short. They needed light and muscle. It was my choice to hold the lights out of the water as other guys assisted in the rescue. It was too late; the boy was dead. Not a burn mark visible; smoke and heat got him, with a window just a couple of feet away. Peggy was still alive as they carried her by me. The scene was utter pandemonium; men silhouetted in my light were yelling and tripping as we tried to intervene on the inevitable. She was outside and being transported.

The fire was extinguished and cleanup underway. Probably within a half hour, life had changed to death. For what? A floor heater and a motorcycle gas tank... *Crazy kids, you should have known better.* No smoke detector. As I look at where Peggy was laying, it seems clear that she got up hearing the boys running to the back side of the house. She must have opened the sliders not knowing that the main fire was on the other side. That's where she dropped, just two feet from a window opening and safety. The next day we heard that Peggy needed blood; we more than filled the request. That's also what firefighters do. She only lived a couple of weeks. So close, yet another tragedy.

Al looks at me as if to say,
"You've finally lost it!"

Underwear and Air Horns in the Night
(What's that Sound?)

Station Three, Mid-1980's, 1:30 a.m.

Captain Al Ramos was in command, with me driving Engine Three. Captain Corny Hall, on Engine Five, was working a trade. The strangest occurrence of my career happened. All was quiet, except for obligatory snoring. For some unknown reason, Engine Three's air horn decided to sound. At first we couldn't understand what this noise was as the sound seemed to be coming from the ceiling and walls. We found ourselves standing in the hallway in our underwear, looking at each other in utter disbelief. I went to Engine Three's apparatus room and found the problem... the air horn happily blaring away. At first I thought it was a joke and expected one of the guys to be crouched on the floorboard honking the horn. As I arrived behind the wheel with sleep in my eyes, in total confusion, the horn stopped. *No reason. Oh well, it stopped. Back to bed... Dummy! I didn't check the air pressure.*

Two a.m. – dispatch tone alert: **"Attention all stations. We have the report of a three-story building on fire at Oak and Alameda Avenue, old Lola's Chicken Restaurant and assorted shops, flames showing from the third story."**

That would be a full response: Engine One, Truck One, Engine Three, and Engine Five. I hit the floor running and moved to Engine Three.

As I turned the ignition, I heard Chief March say, "We have a fully involved three-story building; send a second alarm, Engine Four and Truck Two."

I started the rig and realized that the air pressure was at zero. Captain Al jumped in and said, "Let's go!"

I blurted out, "The air has bled off and the brakes won't release." Then as the air started to build, I knew what the problem was with the horn; it only stopped blowing because the air had bled off. Now, as pressure increased, the horn resumed blowing.

Al looked at me as if to say, "You've finally lost it!"

I screamed to him, "It's not me! It's the d#@ horn. It's stuck!"

By now the chief is announcing for Engine Three to lay a supply line and we're still in the barn, twenty blocks away, lights on, air horn currently at full volume, me pounding on the button to no avail.

Al shouted, "To hell with it! Let's go!"

The scene in the cab was hilarious looking back: Al yelling, the radio pleading, and me driving, pounding, and pulling on the horn button. About half-way down Central, with one final adrenalin-filled pull, the button came off in my hand with spring flying and Al ducking. Yet the horn continued and Al persistently shook his

121

head while he planned his fire attack. At Oak Street, we turned right and, in the headlights a half-block down, was Engine One with Dave at the pump. He was already ankle deep in water with all hose lines off. Truck One was setting up its aerial ladder. Engine Five arrived behind us with three stories of building that took up a quarter of the block, belching flames and smoke.

Then there was our horn, coming straight at him. The look on his face was priceless: *Are you nuts? Have you lost your mind?* We pulled up within a hundred feet of him with horn screaming. All I could think to do was crawl under the rig and, with my adrenalin-charged strength, rammed a Maglight in the bell of the horn. Now it sounded like a squealing pig but much quieter. The brakes were trying to lock up but I managed, with clutch slipping, to force it over to a hydrant where it stayed for the duration of the fire, pumping and squealing until the city mechanic arrived to silence it. I know that, forever, they will think I did something to that horn, but I swear I didn't.

Can We See the Three-Legged Dog?

LeMoine Home, 3219 Thompson Avenue, 5:00 p.m.

My younger daughter had been volunteering at the Alameda City Pound after school. She has always been an animal lover. Bree sat down at the table with that look on her face, like D-a-a-d you're my hero, you're so strong and such a great dad.

She began, "D-a-a-d, I took care of the cutest puppy today."

"No!"

"He was so sweet!"

"No, Bree, we have a hamster, bird, chinchilla, and a dog. I'm sorry, but that's enough."

"But, D-a-a-d, he only has three legs and nobody will save him; he'll be put to sleep. Please just go down to the pound and look at him. Please?"

"Okay, Bree, if we go inspecting tomorrow at the fire department and the captain agrees, I'll try, but we don't need another dog, even if he had just one leg."

"Thanks, Daddy! You're the best."

The next day, late afternoon, somewhere on Buena Vista Avenue we were returning to Station Three. With morning training, lunch, and three hours of inspections out of the way, Captain Ramos said, "Let's go home and have dinner."

Al is a great kidder and always tried to mess with my head, so I thought it might be payback time.

"Hey, Cap, do you think we could stop at the pound on the way back to the station?"

"Why?"

"I need to see a three-legged dog."

Silence, then with a look on his face which says, *What did you say? It must be the roar of the engine; I surely didn't hear what I think I heard.*

"Could we see the three-legged dog?"

Al, with a smirk on his face, responded, "Why sure, I would love to see a three-legged dog."

So off we went with him wondering what I had up my sleeve. Upon arrival at the pound, Al and I got out of the rig and started for the front door.

Firefighter Jim Johnson alongside, asked the captain, "Hey, Al, why are we stopping here?"

Al, now fully hooked and wondering what I was doing, poked Jim in the side and answered, "We had to stop for a minute to see a three-legged dog. Ha ha!"

Now Jim thought we were both crazy, but that's nothing new. So the three of us walked side by side through the doors and up to the counter. Al was thinking this was insane but he was going through with it. Then, the *piece de resistance*:

The shelter mistress came to the counter and greeted us, asking, "Can I help you guys?"

I looked at Al and Jim, then back to her, and asked, "Can we see your three-legged dog?"

Without skipping a beat she replied, "Sure, come right this way; he's in the back."

If I could have put a dollar value on their expressions and sold it, I would have retired right then. So we walked back into the cages looking for the puppy. I thought that Al was thinking this was the greatest setup ever, and somehow the mistress and I were in cahoots, but he was playing along. After looking in all the cages, the dog was nowhere to be found. Al, with a smile, thinks *now I've got them.*

As Al is thinking it's just a rouse, the mistress called up front on the intercom to her helper, "Hey, Alice, you seen the three-legged dog?"

"Yeah," came the reply, "We sold him this morning."

Color left Al's face and he said, "That was good. You're the king. I give up. You're the greatest."

To this day there is a question in Al's mind, *was there ever a three-legged dog?*

I find myself looking into the vacant eyes of a seven year old boy covered with soot, steam rising from his pants.

We Saved Six that Day
(Or a Purpose-Driven Life)

Alameda Times-Star, Wednesday, January 25, 1984

(Editor's note: In the wake of the near fatal fire Tuesday at 2519 Eagle Avenue, involving two adults and four children, firefighter Dave LeMoine wrote this eye witness account of the rescue. Three of the children are still in guarded, but stable condition. The cause of the blaze is still under investigation. The following was written the day of the fire.)

I am writing this for myself and my fellow firefighters to relieve and express some of the emotions we have undergone in the last seven hours today. I am also praying for four little boys, ages 1-1/2, 2-1/2, 4 and 7, their mother and stepfather. This morning at 7:50, I arrived at Fire Station Three to serve my 24-hour tour of

I Could Have Died A Thousand Deaths

duty. Fifty minutes later, I found myself sitting in the back of our ambulance; my feet braced against the sidewall, looking into the vacant eyes of a 7 year old boy. He was desperately struggling to get a breath every 15 seconds. As I looked around the inside of the van, Mike Hoag was holding a 2-1/2 year old boy; next to him, Mark Kroger had a 1-1/2 year old. Both children were laboring to breathe and fighting to live.

In the front seat, Kirk Bell had a 4 year old boy, and was telling Captain Helms, the driver, "I'm running out of 0-2 (oxygen). Can anyone spare a breathing mask?" No one could.

Backtracking a little, Engine Three, with me driving, had arrived second at the fire scene about 8:25. Smoke and flames were breaking out the front windows. My job was to hook up to the hydrant and supply Engine One at the fire. My crew did this with much difficulty due to people who had stopped their cars in the intersection and left them blocking the hydrant. I could see down the block the worst fear a firefighter has: children being carried out of the building. I wanted to run to their aid, but knew my job was to stay by the pump. I heard an urgent cry on the radio for another resuscitator. There was no one to get it so I did what an engineer should never do; I left the engine pumping on its own. A quick check of the rig and I ran to the scene with the breathing equipment. There seemed to be kids all over the place. I knelt down by the 7 year old boy; his clothes were steaming and black-ened with soot.

I asked Doug, "Is the boy breathing?"

Doug wasn't sure, "Maybe every 30 seconds," he responded.

As Doug and I worked on the boy, I glanced around to see six victims, two firefighters frantically working on each of the boys

126

and three firefighters each on the adults. One firefighter was operating Engine One, and two were trying to find a fifth child who
might still be inside. I looked up at the building and the fire was
starting to engulf the front window again. There was no one to man
the hose lines. Chief Cowell was calling for a second alarm with
Rescue 32 ambulance. We needed more manpower. At this point,
the building wasn't important except that the fire could extend to
the house next door.

Captain Helms made the decision that we could not wait any
longer for the ambulance. We each grabbed a child and piled into
the van.

As I climbed in with my child, I yelled at the chief, "No one is
running my engine!"

He said it could not be helped and to go on to the hospital. It
seemed like an eternity to arrive at Alameda Hospital though we
broke all records getting there. On the way, it was crazy looking
out the window at people driving their cars not even heeding the
sirens. They didn't seem to care. Yet inside the van, four kids were
fighting for their lives. Alameda Hospital had been alerted of our
plight. We moved the four boys into a common room. Throughout
the next hour, we firefighter-emergency medical technicians assisted the medical staff. There is no way I could explain that hour
except to say, you had to have been there. In all the turmoil, there
was a beautiful order. Two of the children started crying, which
was a joy to hear. The other two were still vacant-eyed but breathing better on intubations and 0-2. By this time, a fifth victim, a
man, had been brought in and, in his delirium, it took six of us to
hold him down.

All of a sudden I was not needed anymore. Hardly 1-½ hours had
gone by, but it seemed like 2 days. As I stood at the foot of the 4

127

year old's bed, the thought hit me, *how frail the human being is.* "Oh, God," I said under my breath. I made my way to the privacy of the bathroom where tears welled up and emotions overwhelmed me. On that gurney I had seen my children and your children. I thought, this could have been avoided by the purchase of a $10 smoke detector. When will the people learn? Don't wait for your landlord to buy one; save yourself!

Back to the fire; it was under control; time to pick up the hose. Ed Smith had come in off duty, on his own, to run my rig. That's how firemen are. Time to clean up and to get ready for the next fire. It will come. I have been a firefighter for 15 years. I've lived this scene many times before, not always with the intensity of today, but sometimes worse. It is now 4:15 p.m. I have escaped the activity of the dayroom to my bunk. The warm afternoon sun is calming and the room is quiet as I write. Good news has just arrived; all four boys are in guarded but stable condition and have been transferred to Children's Hospital. When you see the fire on the news tonight, they will give it about 30 seconds; and on to the price of corn in Nebraska, Middle East war, or the local sports scores, but I know that six people are alive today because of men of <u>uncommon valor</u> and love for this city and its residents. I love this job!

Dave LeMoine, Engineer

The Catapult
(Or How to Clean the Undercarriage the Hard Way)

Station One, Early Seventies, Early Morning

Engine One, Captain Steckler is the officer, with Ed driving and me on the tailboard. Truck One, Lieutenant Ray Hutton, with Otis

128

driving and Moe on the back, or should I say side. The real Truck One was out of service and in its place, our old, antiquated reserve utility truck. It was a 1953 White cab-over, no aerial ladder, with a gutless, underpowered gasoline flathead with 6 cylinders, manual choke, and a terrible 5-speed transmission. There were no jump seats so the firefighter had to stand on the side holding onto the bar. You could see everything ahead of you, but with no protection. The highest thing on the rig tonight was Moe's head. If Otis slammed on the brakes you could watch Moe fly over the cab, land on the street in front of the rig with just enough time to be run over. If the driver was good, and there was enough clearance, and if you stayed flat, you might be able to check the undercarriage as it rolled over you. It could be a good vantage point to see if the driver had cleaned the frame that day.

What are My Legs Doing in My Sweatshirt?
(Or You Had to Have Been There to Believe it)

Station One, Mid-1980's, 2:30 a.m.

"A" Shift was on duty, Bill Simon dispatching. We firefighters would stand three-hour watches at the switchboard from noon through nine p.m. and then, in rotation, sleep in the watch room through the night... we hoped. Bill would take over if a call came in; otherwise he slept in the dorm with the rest of us. At midnight, all were asleep when we heard the tone alert and the lights drop (turn on).

"Attention all stations! We have the report of a house fire on Bay Farm Island, Engine Five from Station Four, Fountain and Jackson with Truck One."

I Could Have Died A Thousand Deaths

In these years, we all had to bunk (get dressed) whether dispatched or not. We reported to the dispatch room until the all clear. If you weren't responding, you would let the crew that was responding bunk first, and you would take your time. Knowing Truck One was going to the fire, I looked across the dorm and noticed that Otis was sitting on the side of the bed with a puzzled look on his face. He was holding his sweatshirt up and studying it. Usually he was first out the door.

I yelled, "Otis! The call's for you! Otis!"

He didn't respond. All the rest of the crew was out of the dorm, and there he sat.

"Otis!"

He then started to put his foot into his sweatshirt and pull. The guy was still asleep!

"Otis!"

I got to him as he was coming to. Now he looked in disbelief at what he was doing, wondering how the sweatshirt got on his legs. I pulled it off, he bunked and I directed him toward the door and down the stairs, not sure that he was awake yet. He moved on his own toward the truck, and I entered the dispatch room. Now it really got good. Bill was at the console but still half asleep himself. He had already gotten a reply from Lt. Hutton that Truck One was responding. He assumed that the truck was out the door. I looked through the apparatus room window and saw that Moe was on the side, Ray was in the cab, and Otis was still staggering toward the rig. Bill had been doing this job so long that he did everything by braille. The truck was just starting to move when, to my amazement, Bill, thinking by now that the truck, as usual, should be on the street, reached up and, without looking, hit the button to close the door. The door started to come down as the cab was passing under; I doubt that Otis or Ray were even aware, but Moe was.

I screamed, "Bill!"

Moe has now ducked below his knuckles, which were the highest thing on the truck. He was looking up in disbelief. The door continued, the truck continued, and Moe continued, but I had stopped breathing. I can see, in my mind's eye, the door scattered all over the ground with Chief Magby in his rough voice asking, *"W-h-y?"* It's hard to believe as I stood there frozen, but the door cleared by about six inches and Otis drove merrily down the street, unaware that anything was different. Moe thought to himself, *I need to get back and change my shorts.* We trained and we trained but it only takes one thing out of order to muck up the situation.

Code Blue at the Curb
(The Baby's Color is Good but He's Unresponsive)

Station One, 6:00 a.m.

We woke to the tone alert; just two more hours and I'd be off duty. Hope it's not a medical call. But that time of the morning it always is.

"Attention all stations! We have the report of a child not breathing at 1212 Park Avenue. This will be a still response for Rescue 31."

Oh, man, it was for us. It was only a block away; as we approached we saw a woman in the headlights standing at the curb with a small bundle in her arms. I stepped out of the ambulance and she handed the baby to me and said, "He's not breathing." Without a second thought, the woman was strapped into the passenger seat, as I climbed in the back with the baby, Dave driving and Jim alongside. I had a good air exchange going but he was still unconscious. One minute later, at Alameda Emergency, we handed him off to the medical staff. Sometimes I hated this job, but then it's in my blood to be in the middle of things. It seemed like all the nurses and doctors on call appeared. The baby's color was good but he was non-responsive. An hour went by with no change, although everyone was doing their best. Then the thought came, *What about the parents in the waiting room being neglected because all of our focus is on their child?* I thought of my children at home safe in bed while this family was being torn. I went to talk to them about the progress.

Entering the waiting room, hardly knowing what they looked like because we had been so focused on their son, I scanned the room. Still not sure, they recognized me, the one they had entrusted the life of their son to. The mother moved quickly toward me; the father was still in a daze. As she drew near and I saw her eyes, her emotion triggered mine; we found ourselves crying and embracing. I told them that the doctors were doing everything they could, but there was no news yet.

I found myself asking, "Would you like me to pray for you?"

She nodded, "Please do." So I prayed with the urgency we were all feeling.

As I headed back to the trauma room, a nurse was passing to talk to the parents. She told me it was another SIDS. I already knew, Sudden Infant Death Syndrome. *I don't understand, Lord. He was such a beautiful baby,* I thought. Back at the station, I called the

SIDS Center and they assured me they would send a counselor to help the family.

Eight a.m., I was off duty and on the way home to hug my wife and daughters. Passing by Park Avenue, I stopped out front but couldn't seem to leave. The thought came to mind to go to the door and try to say something, anything, to let the couple know it isn't just another day in a fireman's life but it was now my child too. I didn't know what to do with the grief. I felt like an invader in what should have been a private time of mourning. But, to my surprise, as they opened the door, they were at peace and seemed pleased to see me.

"I'm so sorry for your loss. What can I do?"

"You're so kind," came the reply. "We're okay. It was God's will."

How did I share what just happened with my own family? I couldn't. So I stuffed it, and tried to mow the lawn.

Eight months later, at my desk in the lieutenant's room, Station One, 3:00 p.m., a call came over the intercom, "Lt. LeMoine, you have a visitor up front." As I entered the front room, I saw the father of the little boy; he was smiling and greeted me with a warm handshake.

"Dave, I just wanted you to know that we are doing great. The SIDS counselor helped, but God and your prayer helped more. We went through our grief together and are at peace. My wife is pregnant and expecting soon. Thank you."

"No," I replied. "Thank *you* for teaching me how to go through the most terrible trial without blaming God. I truly have seen a miracle." I learned that, when God closes one small door, He opens a highway.

The Fireboat is Sinking
(Is That Water in the Cabin?)

September 1989 - Closing Day of Yacht Season

It was a beautiful fall Sunday afternoon and, here we were, another 24 hour shift at Station Three. Our fireboat was just sitting alone in the Marina itching to be cruising the waters around town. Alameda is an island surrounded with Navy and civilian ships, barges, marinas and creosoted piers just waiting to burn. I had worked my way into "A" Shift Boat Trainer, a position which gave me some pull to spend more time doing the job I loved. From childhood, having grown up boating, fishing, and water skiing in these waters, I knew most of the sunken hazards, tidal currents, and mud flats to be maneuvered.

Picking up the phone, I called the shift commander at Station One asking him to check with the duty chief, to see if we could run the boat this afternoon to improve our skill. The reply was affirmative; maybe I should have felt a little guilty, but Neptune was calling. What the chief didn't know was that there were thousands of boats out for the final day of yacht season, decorated with flags, streamers and people. We joined in the celebration, our boat shooting streams of water from all truants at every conceivable type of water craft, with people waving, bikini clad girls smiling, and teasing the three uniformed studs. Our normal boundaries were from the San Leandro Bay to the mouth of the estuary. Arriving at San Francisco Bay, all these boats were leaving us as our leash became tight. We cruised back and forth as our boat seemed to be straining at its tether. It was more than three red-blooded men could handle. The pull was magnetic. I could swear I heard the water say *"You know, there's not a wave in site and your boat really needs to be run hard, to blow out the carbon."*

"Hey guys, let's just run out to the end of the channel marker."

It seemed good, and I swore the guys to a blood oath of silence. We're off to the last buoy. "That was fast, do you suppose we could just go as far as Yerba Buena Island? I'm sure we can get back fast if a call comes in." *Hmm, that was easy,* as I think to myself, *What if we circumnavigate Yerba Buena? The boat is running great, the tanks are full. What could possibly go wrong? Besides, who's gonna know?*

Yeah, right. With the thousands of boats out today, who's going to know? What if the chief of the department just happened to be on one of the boats waving at us? Is our job really worth that little? Hmm, at this minute, with the sea calling and brains saturated with salt water, we'll be okay. Full throttle ahead! As we disappeared around the lee side of the island, I admit to thinking, *I do have a wife and kids, a mortgage, and what **was** a great job. I think I'll hold my breath until we arrive back at that now-distant channel marker. Boat, don't fail me now.* As we passed that beautiful channel buoy I think to myself *that was really dumb! Maybe they should make a movie about us called "Dumb and Dumber."*

With our fun winding down, and back home in the channel still afloat, we returned to a normal patrol while the boat settled into a slow idle. I was at the wheel and calmly returned to waving and looking. In my day-dreaming state, something seemed different about the boat… it was sitting lower in the water. As my eyes focused ahead, I could see the bow wake showing a little above the deck. That was not good.

"Hey guys, does something seem different about the boat?"

I opened the cabin door and stepped down into two feet of water. I couldn't believe what I was seeing and feeling. Apparently the boat, under full power, was bow high as we cruised around the bay. The force of the high speed had opened a seam in the keel and it started taking on water, which moved to the stern. As we slowed in the estuary, the water started running forward which caused the boat to be nose heavy. Now the bow was tilting lower than the stern and that was not normal. We had 30 feet of water below and, yeah, it was warm but I hadn't packed my trunks.

Yelling to the crew, "We're sinking! Get the syphon hose out and hook it to the pump! We'll try to rescue our own boat. That's a first!" The guys had never tested the syphon. Luckily, I had. "Hook it to number two discharge and start the engine." I grabbed the radio trying to be cool, "Fireboat to Central."

"Central, go ahead."

"We are in the estuary near the Rusty Pelican and about to sink." I think, *if the pump doesn't work, we'll have to beach it in the mud, which will make my name Lt. Mud for the rest of my very short career.* I was hoping for an open boat slip. "Could you dispatch Truck Two with the portable pump? We need them now."

"Roger, fireboat can you give us your exact location?"

"Well, we will either be in the Rusty Pelican marina or on the bottom of the bay!"

"Roger!"

The pump engine actually started, which was a miracle in itself, and water started to flow out of the boat which was a good thing; we just might make it. *Ah, yachting. Isn't life grand?* With water now spraying out of the syphon hose and irritating passing boats, we pulled into an open slip but we were still not out of the woods. We were not sure how much water was coming in and if our pump would handle it. Truck Two arrived, pump in hand, and we started making headway. Then a crowd gathered, including the duty chief, to see what all the commotion was about. As I pondered, *do I tell him the whole truth or just trim it to the bare essentials? I think I'll go for the bare essentials.*

As long as the chief wasn't on a boat in the bay and none of the 20,000 boaters turned us in, what could happen? Between the two pumps, we were able to dry out the bilges to see that the leak was small. The chief decided to have us take the boat to the shipyard and put it on the ways. Our job was to hold our breath, move slow with the portable pump on board, and hope for the best. We did, it did, and we became heroes for saving the boat, at least for the moment. That was, if I believed a firefighter could keep a secret. With relief, looking back thirty years, our secret was kept and I got my retirement. Sometimes we receive wisdom from wise people, sometimes from life experiences, and sometimes from a swift kick in the butt. Whatever works and, in this case, that mistake was never repeated.

Many times in the past, rolling up on an emergency (be it fire, car accident, broken leg, or a child with his head stuck in a railing), after evaluating and fixing the need, we might ask the question, "What were you thinking?" *That was really dumb!* From now on I won't be so quick to judge, having moved into the same category as the civilians we served. We live and sometimes we die. This is what my job was about…helping people, and sometimes even helping ourselves.

Times-Star Newspaper Account
Of a Police Action

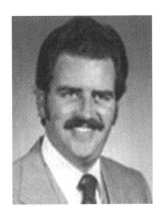

Officer Robert James Davey, Jr.
Alameda Police Department
California
End of Watch: Thursday, March 3, 1983
Cause: Gunfire

Biographical Info
Age: 33
Tour of Duty: 10 years
Badge Number: 76

Officer Robert Davey was shot and killed while assisting members of his department conduct a drug raid on a home. He had just finished his normal shift and was not part of the raiding team, but assisted when they asked at the last moment. He was positioned at the rear of the home. As the six members of the team entered through the front, one of the drug dealer's bodyguards jumped through a side window carrying an AR-15 that had been modified to a fully automatic M-16. Officer Davey ordered the man to drop his weapon but the man opened fire, striking Officer Davey in the side. Officer Davey returned fire, striking the suspect in the chest several times.

Before succumbing to his wounds, Officer Davey was able to secure the rifle so that the suspect could not fire at other officers. The suspect was taken into custody in the backyard.

Officer Davey had been a member of the Alameda Police Department for just over ten years, and is survived by his wife and four children.

As I moved past the window, I can hear crashing and yelling above my head. What are we doing in the middle of a drug raid?

Shots Fired - Officer Down

Station Three - 1983, 5:00 p.m.

I was driving Engine Three, working with Captain Cornelius Hall and firefighter Jim. The time was around 5:00 p.m.; we were looking forward to a nice dinner and some good fellowship... but not yet. That too-familiar sound breaks the quiet, the tone alert. *Not now. Our dinner will get cold!*

"Attention all stations. We have the report of shots fired. Officer down in the ten hundred block of Central Avenue. That will be a still response for Engine Three and Rescue Two."

I Could Have Died A Thousand Deaths

Here comes the adrenalin, maybe two minutes into the response, just a block away from the scene, Corney was on the radio to Central trying to get more information.

"What are we in for?" I asked.

"No further info at this time."

As we approached, we could see maybe ten squad cars, cops in flack vests, with shotguns and assault weapons. I hoped they had it under control. Upon arrival, Captain Hall and Jim were told to enter the house. I was to stand by the rig for further instructions.

As the two firefighters ran up the stairs led by Alameda Police Department (APD), another officer came out from beside the building and yelled to me, "He's back here!"

Moving onto the path next to the house, I realized I had been left alone...not a good feeling. The path was maybe four feet wide from the house to the fence. As I passed the window, I could hear crashing and yelling above my head inside the building. Ahead of me, the sidewalk was covered with glass. Looking past it, I could see Rob lying face down at the back corner with his head toward me. I was alone, wondering where the cops were, and what was in the backyard. Slowly, I looked around the corner and was shocked to see four or five police on the other side of the yard. No one was near Rob.

Someone yelled at me to do something. As I rolled Rob on his back, I saw the AR-15 under him. He was unresponsive and code blue. Corney and Jim arrived. We tried to start CPR but were having trouble, being hindered by his flak vest. Try as we might, we couldn't seem to remove it. Everything we did seemed dreamlike, as if moving in slow motion. Rescue Two arrived and we decided instantly to scoop and run in hopes that the doctors at Alameda Emergency could do a miracle. With one motion, Rob was lifted to the gurney and rolled toward the ambulance. We had a clear airway, no pulse and were attempting CPR in too narrow of a path but it was the only way out. Corney and Jim got into the ambulance with Rescue Two's crew. I closed the door and watched them disappear into the dusk.

It was strangely quiet for just a moment. Then another cop ran up and said, "You'd better come to the backyard again! We have the suspect with three bullet holes in him."

Great! I was the only firefighter there and didn't have much faith that the APD would help. I called, "Central, could you dispatch Rescue One? We have another shooting victim."

"Roger. Rescue One en route."

I then grabbed what was left of the medical supplies and followed a shotgun-toting officer back to the rear yard. The scene is still etched in my memory. There was one policeman alongside me and three standing on the east side of the yard near the house. I heard shouting but saw no assailant. I asked, "Where is he?"

The policeman pointed to the rear of the yard behind a hedge. By now, I had no confidence in the police and wished someone would explain what was going on. I heard yelling but didn't have the foggiest idea what or where the man was, or if he was still armed.

The cop seemed dazed, as he motioned to me again and said, "Around here."

Behind the hedge was a man facedown with handcuffs and three 357 bullets in him. He was still screaming, "Kill me! Kill me!"

I Could Have Died A Thousand Deaths

Three cops were standing over him. They had purposely said nothing to us about him until Rob had been attended to. As I began to triage, Rescue One arrived. With a sigh of relief, I handed off to them and made a beeline for Alameda Emergency.

As I walked into the trauma room, it seemed like every nurse and doctor in the hospital was there. Corney was doing heart compression. I asked if he needed a break. He didn't, so I backed up against the wall just as the cardiologist asked Corney, "Do you have a squeamish stomach?"

He replied, "No."

In seconds, with one swipe of the scalpel into Rob's left side, the doctor spread the ribs just enough to get his hand in to feel the heart. The doctor said, "No blood in the heart and the aorta is shredded. Nothing more can be done."

Why? It made no sense. Thinking back to the scene, I was puzzled about how the gun got under Rob. What must have happened, as Rob was positioned at the southwest corner of the building looking into the backyard, he was watching the door with his back to the side path. When the cops entered the front door, the assailant jumped through the west side window and landed on the path facing Rob. Both men must have been startled and, facing each other, they fired. Rob hit the man three times; unfortunately, though he was hit only once, the bullet just nicked his vest and entered under his arm. One inch either way might have saved his life.

They must have come together and Rob was able to wrestle the gun away before falling, which probably saved some of his fellow officers. The drugged up crazy made it to the backyard with three 357 bullets in him. What a shame he lived; frankly, I didn't want to

142

touch him and was glad to step back as help arrived that hadn't seen what he had done to our brother. No more dad, no more husband, and no more friend.

A couple of days later, Assistant Chief Alberty interviewed all firefighters that responded to the shooting. It seems that we received a report from APD that the fire department was slow and inept with our performance at the scene. Upon hearing that, I blew up and told him that the only thing that wasn't done right at the scene was on the part of the cops. It must be their cover-up for doing nothing. It was simply a smokescreen to divert attention from their guilty conscience. I offered to testify to what really went down, and nothing more was said. In hindsight, it's hard to deal with one of your own, and the fact that it could have been any one of them, caused the avoidance. I do understand. Shock can do that.

Station Four, Bay Farm Island – 1992
(Sir, Step Out of the Car)

The Report of a Car Versus Building, 801 Island Drive

Another quiet afternoon on Harbor Bay Isle around 4:00 p.m.

"Attention all stations! We have a still alarm for Engine Four to 801 Island Drive, the Water's Edge Retirement Home. The report of a car inside an apartment."

"Engine Four responding. Did you say, 'a car inside a garage'?"

"Central. No, a car has crashed through a wall into a lower apartment."

I Could Have Died A Thousand Deaths

"Roger. Engine Four on the scene."

Pulling into the driveway, we saw a small group of seniors standing together on the sidewalk. Scanning the building, I couldn't seem to find a car near, up against, or sticking out of the building. A couple of people were pointing toward the right. I told Don, our driver, to wait there until I checked with the crowd. As I approached the group, I asked if they had seen a car hit a building.

"Yes, over there to the right, where we were pointing."

I think to myself, *they are seniors and must be a little nuts, or I'm blind, but I don't see a thing.*

One of the men said, "Son, look closer at that apartment."

I looked and saw some cracked siding, but no car.

"Young man, walk over there and look in the window! Yeah, look through the window."

Now I knew it was a joke. To humor them, I walked onto the grass and saw some tire tracks in the lawn leading up to the side wall. I thought the car must have hit the wall and left the scene.

Then a slightly perturbed senior said, "Come over here. Look through the window!"

No, it couldn't be. I'm seeing things. Is that a trunk lid in the front room? Looking closer, through the living room window, I saw a car sitting in a studio apartment with no apparent way it could have gotten in there. The apartments in that section only had one way in and out, through a hallway door. Seemingly, the only way for something that big to get in was to dematerialize and reappear on the living room rug.

I called for the crew and entered through the hallway, then opened the door which stopped up against the front bumper of a four-door sedan. There sat a man with a puzzled look on his face, still in the driver's seat.

"Alameda Fire here. Sir, step out of the car. Are you okay?"

"Yes, I think so, but how did I get in here?"

Apparently he was parking in front of his own apartment when he stepped on the gas instead of the brake. The car went airborne, through a hedge, across the lawn, and hit his own apartment wall dead center. If he had been in any one of twenty other parking places, he could have jumped the hedge, cleared the lawn, and crushed Grandma Moses watching Oprah in her rocking chair! The wall broke along the bottom and two sides. Still hanging from the ceiling, it acted like a hinge. The wall then moved inward and up just enough for the car to pass through, sliding to a stop at his kitchen sink. The sink was still intact, and the car was just far enough into the room to allow the wall to return to its prior position without even breaking a window.

We retrieved the man unscratched, called a carpenter to remove the newly crafted garage door, then a tow truck to extract the culprit vehicle, and finally went to dinner thinking *no one will ever believe this!*

The Chest

1997 - Retired Three Years, and Living in Redding

I received a call from Assistant Chief Pogue, who had just retired. He says, "Hi Dave. Are you coming to Alameda in the near future?"

145

I Could Have Died A Thousand Deaths

I responded, "Yes, in a couple of weeks. Why?"

"I have something I think you would like. Call me when you get in so we can meet."

Two weeks later, I'm at Bob's door. "Hi Dave. Come in and take a look at this chest."

Before me is a small, old looking, homemade, four-drawer chest.

Bob said, "I inherited this thing when I joined the department in  1965. I didn't know where it came from, but it was in my locker so I kept it through my 30 years. On retirement, the box was too much of an old friend to leave behind, so I brought it home and sat it up on a garage shelf. Now, I have had it for over thirty years but never took the time to examine it. I just used it for my socks and extra clothing."

My part of the story is: I joined the department three years after Bob and retired two years before he did. I probably passed his opened locker throughout my career 10,000 times but never saw this chest in my life.

"It looks interesting, Bob, but what caused you to want to show it to me at this late date?"

Bob continued his story, "I had a tractor for sale and two men came to my garage to look at it. As we talked, one of the men saw the chest and asked if I would sell it."

"Not a chance! It's an old friend," Bob responded.

"Can I look at it? Where did you get it? It looks old. What's it made of?" this stranger inquired.

Bob continued, "So I brought it to the bench for closer examination. The man had an eye for old furniture and, as we looked closer, we could see that it had been made from old orange crates. Inside, and on the back of one of the drawers, was stamped "Piggly Wiggly Grocery" and some other logos. Looking further, under one of the small drawers, in pencil, was a faint signature of the builder, and that's why I called you."

Bob proceeded to pull out the left front drawer and turn it over.

"Take a look at the signature, Dave! It will blow your socks off!"

My eyes adjusted to the faint pencil signature, and I was shocked to see "*Jack LeMoine - 1942*" written in a distinct, cursive hand. I gasped, realizing Dad made this chest in 1942. He died in 1949, and his chest stayed as a resident in the station for over 55 years. None of my family had a clue of its existence. Apparently its ownership had been lost over the many years, as dad had died suddenly of a heart attack and never returned to claim it. I was eight when he died, but remembered him as a kind, caring father. He is the reason I was, and always will be, a firefighter. Gratefully, the chest returned home to live in my family.

I Could Have Died A Thousand Deaths

Dad and Mrs. Lane on Bay Farm Island

Not Really a Witch

The year was about 1953. I was 12 years old; Jim was 8. Dad had died in 1949. I missed him very much. Even though the firefighters had tried to take over, the eight years of our life together could not be replaced. A great emptiness was in my gut; I couldn't shake it.

We lived next to Godfrey Park and on the other side of the park was a great grape stake fence, probably 9 feet tall. Behind the fence lived an old lady named Mrs. Lane. "Old Lady Lane," as we called her, lived by herself on about two acres surrounded by the fence. The kids at play in the park would often go to the fence and peak through the cracks. All kinds of rumors ran wild about her being a witch that ate little children. The yard was mostly very tall weeds but she also had a vegetable garden and fruit trees. Twenty or more half-wild cats roamed the yard with goats, ducks and rabbits. The house was shack-like with an old car in the shed, though we never saw her drive it. Mrs. Lane was slight of build, maybe 85 pounds. She had one kind of clothing, a black dress and wide-brimmed black hat, with heavy tan nylons rolled down below her knees.

Sometimes she would sneak up on us and yell, "Go away!" We made fun of her, though my conscience would make me go easier than most of the kids. I actually felt sorry for her; she only wanted to be left alone. Dad and Mom had raised me to respect elders and I knew better.

One early summer morning, being so close to the park, Jim and I were the only two kids there. I could see Mrs. Lane way across the lawn, raking the grass cuttings into a wheelbarrow. With Jim in tow and a little nervous, I walked over, said hello, picked up her rake, and helped load grass. At this closer distance, she looked more like an 80 pound grandma than a witch. Jim pitched in and, in no time, I was wheeling a full load to her back gate. Our conversation consisted mostly of,

"You're the LeMoine boys, aren't you?"

"Yes."

"Your father was a good man."

"You knew my dad?"

"Yes. One day years ago, my car had broken down, and I asked him for help. Though very busy building your house, he dropped everything to help me. He was a great man."

"Thank you for telling me that. I had no idea."

"Would you and your brother like to have a new kitten?"

"Yes, but I need to ask Mom."

"You do that, and then come and pick out one from the litter."

Fluffy was our kitten's name and she won first place in the park pet show. Mom knitted her a hat and our picture was on the front page of the _Times-Star_, Fluffy sitting on my head with said hat. From then on, Jim and I defended and respected Mrs. Lane. We left her to her yard, but I would always look across the park to see if she needed help. My dad left us a wonderful heritage. Long after he was gone, his reputation lives on. This story is just one of many of the legacies of Mom and Dad.

I Could Have Died A Thousand Deaths

<u>The Heritage Continues</u>

<u>Morning Song – November 8, 2000</u>

Patty and I had flown down to Pismo Beach that morning to stay at my sister-in-law's home. We arrived about ten a.m. I was sitting at the piano as I often do, just fooling around, when this lovely melody came to me. The warm sun was shining through the window and everything seemed right with the world.

Patty came down the stairs and asked, "Is that new? I don't think I've heard it before."

"Yeah," I replied. "It just came to me. I think I'll keep it, my first composition."

"What are you going to name it?" she asked.

"It's such a nice morning, I think I'll name it 'Morning Song.'"

Later, we went out for the afternoon walking on the beach, eating seafood and enjoying the day. At 8:00 p.m. I got a call from Rusty Malone. *What's Brother Jim's best friend calling me for?*

"Hi, Russ. What's up?"

"Dave, it's about Jim. He had a heart attack this morning and didn't make it," was his emotional response.

"What? Not my brother! He trained every day of his life and was in great shape. What happened?"

"He was riding his bike this morning about 10:00 and just fell over on the street. The fire department was called but couldn't save him."

De'ja vu, just like my dad. "Thank you for being the one to break the news, Russ. We'll be on our way to tell Mom and should be there by morning."

We drove all night and talked to Mom early the next day. Jim was greatly honored by Alameda County Fire Department who dedicated the San Leandro fireboat in my brother's name, "The Big Jim LeMoine."

In 2003, I was one of the main speakers at the Sacramento Fire Department Memorial to honor our fallen firefighters. Brother Jim and Dad's names were installed with the hundreds of other heroes, which was quite a tribute. Much later, at home and at the piano again, that melody returned.

Patty posed the question, "Is that the tune you were playing in Pismo?"

"Yeah, I think so."

"What did you name it again?" she questioned.

"I think I called it 'Morning Song.'"

"And, wasn't that about 10:00 a.m.?" Patty probed.

"Uh huh," I responded.

"Isn't that the time your brother died? Maybe it has a double meaning and you didn't even think about it before now. You called it 'Morning Song' and you didn't know that you would be **mourning** your brother's death at that very moment."

"Wow, isn't God good? He was already preparing me for what I would have to do. And then He gave me a song in my heart to comfort and help me remember my Brother Jim."

<u>Last Day on the Job</u>

The date is now January 1, 1994, 8:00 a.m. Those 25 years have come and gone. Too many cups of coffee to count and too many stories to ever record. I think of Frank, long gone from the table, as I wave goodbye to the guys and walk through the dayroom door into a new life. No more sleepless nights or smoke-filled lungs, I am free to find a new adventure. No more late nights with the crew of eight laughing, crying, yelling, and facing whatever comes our way, knowing we're a team, *"a band of brothers."* No more sounds of engine and siren and that, oh too familiar, sound of fire in the walls. Or hose lines filling with water, the screams from a bystander pleading, "There's someone inside!" Now in the parking lot behind the station, I hear Engine One start in the apparatus room for the morning check. As I walk to my car, nothing has changed except... Wow! Now it is *150* years of family fire service, and I'm part of that history!

Last Day
1-1-94

Speech at Firefighter Memorial

Today My Dad and Brother's Names are Being Installed on the Wall – May 22, 2003

I was asked to give a speech at the Capital in Sacramento, California. The event was the Second Annual Fire Department Memorial. Below is the speech in its entirety, though it covers some of what has already been written:

My name is Dave LeMoine, retired lieutenant from the City of Alameda. I've been asked to speak a little of family and the fire service. My story represents thousands of stories, of family, both blood and career. I am a fourth generation firefighter. My great grandfather was chief in Grand Rapids, Michigan for 30 years. He had two sons, one a captain in Michigan, and the other my grandfather. Grandfather retired in 1917 as fire chief of Richmond, California. My uncle, a mechanic for Richmond, put together their first aerial ladder truck. Then he joined the suppression side, and retired as a firefighter. My Dad and brother, two of the men we are

153

I Could Have Died A Thousand Deaths

honoring here today, were engineers. Dad was with Alameda City while my younger brother, Jim, was with Alameda County.

I retired almost 10 years ago as a lieutenant for the City of Alameda after 25 years of service. Most of my career I was a dry foot (engineer), the best job going. Where else could you have the enjoyment of jumping behind the wheel of 20 tons of red iron, with the smell of diesel and the roar of the turbo kicking in... then the added pleasure of seeing little kids smiling and waving as you scream down the streets to your next emergency? As I speak, my nephew, Jason (a trauma nurse), is finishing his training with Alameda County to start the LeMoine's fifth generation. He follows his dad into Alameda County as I followed my dad into Alameda City. One of Jason's chiefs is my godson, David Lord. Jason is in good hands. Family... that's what it's about, both blood and fire service. In my life, I've had one blood brother. In my career I've had some 400 close brothers and sisters. I don't know of any other job in the world where you can know and trust your brothers with your life, or share your deepest and most personal thoughts as you live together 24 hours a day.

When I was a child, my family lived three blocks from Station Three. Mom, my brother, and I would often visit Dad in the evenings. He was my hero! Engine Three and Five's response route to the east end of town often took them within a half-block of our home. Whenever Jim and I heard the sirens, we would jump on our tricycle, me driving with Jim on the tailboard. We would ride as fast as we could to the corner and wave at Dad. I could see him driving and the guys waving back. That's where it all started for Jim and me.

Dad was taken early from this life with a heart attack. I was just 8 and he was 40. I witnessed the AFD resuscitator crew, his brothers, in our living room as they tried in vain to revive him. Pressures

154

from the job wore him out before his time. The pain and memories of that incident framed my life. I lost a dad that day but gained 20 dads for many years to come. Those guys built an addition onto our house, took turns escorting Jim and me to all of the father-and-son school functions, and their families comforted and cared for Mom while we were growing up.

Years passed and, after my schooling, I worked in the trades for a decade, but always felt as if something was missing. One day, I decided to visit my father-in-law, who, you might guess, was a lieutenant in Alameda. It had been 20 years since I had visited Station Three. Upon entering the front door, all of my senses were assaulted as the memories flooded in. The station, built in 1923, smelled of smoke, gasoline, rubber boots, floor wax, musty mops, coffee, and fried chicken. I knew I was home.

One year later I lived there as I began my own, very satisfying, career. What other job is there in the world where you can be sitting around a table eating prime rib, telling stories, and three minutes later be standing in the headlights of your rig, breathing life back into a three month old baby girl? Then, eight years later, while pumping at a fully-involved Victorian fire, be approached by an unfamiliar woman saying, "Dave, you don't know me but I know you. You saved my baby. She and her twin sister are now in third grade and doing great. Thank you!"

Or what other job is there, where you arrive to work at 7:30 a.m. and, by 11:30, all companies in your department have been committed to another house fire. We rescued four children and two adults that day, all struggling to breathe. Then, because we only had one ambulance on scene, four guys with children in their arms crowded in, and continued doing CPR en route to the trauma center, against all protocol. In the hospital, we were assigned ambu bags as the understaffed hospital called for more personnel. I found myself assisting on the four year old. As I worked, my two daughters came to mind. *Come on kid, breathe!* When he started to cry, a cheer exploded in the room. I was quickly pushed out of the way by newly arriving nurses and made my way to the bathroom where it was safe for emotions to burst forth. *Thank You, God!* Three days later they were okay. They all made it.

But, no matter how the day went, there was always chow time, laughter, and family. Sometimes my brother, Jim, would show up to compare stories. Sometimes I would sit in his San Leandro station. No real difference, just family bantering back and forth about life experiences. I lost my dad early and now my brother. I miss them, and miss the endless hours my brother and I had comparing departments. While I bragged about the accomplishments of my department, he was convinced until the day he died that Alameda County was the place to be. They gave him wonderful opportunities to shine there and to use his expertise in waterfront emergency situations. They even honored him by naming a fireboat "The Big Jim LeMoine." The family couldn't be more proud of his accomplishments. We all miss Jim, as I know you miss your loved ones, our fallen heroes. I know I speak for all of us in thanking those who worked so hard to create this beautiful tribute to these well-deserved comrades. And thank you, also, for letting me share a little bit of what it means to be in the firefighting family.

For those of you who are new to the fire service, your memories are just starting. Make the most of them. Your story is just beginning, but your history goes back hundreds of years. Every morning when you arrive at work and are going through another rig check, then mopping the floor, know that you are adding to an unbroken line of wonderful fire service tradition.

Great Grandad

Grandad

Dad

Brother Jim

Me - 1969

I Could Have Died A Thousand Deaths

Porter School

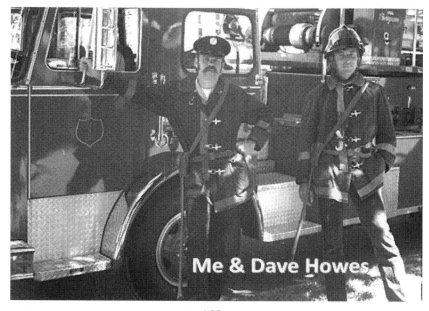

Me & Dave Howes

Dad - Practicing

My First Ship Fire
1969

Mike Long   Archie Bowles   Bobby Weidlich

Yosemite a better way

Yosemite   The Kid

I Could Have Died A Thousand Deaths

Spring activated doors

Ed Kapellas Harry Bass seated, Moe Hale, and Me

1947 Seagrave

PART FOUR
Random Musings and Miscellaneous Memories

Hero on Vacation
(Or "Another Kind of Fireboat")

Ten Miles Off the Coast of San Simeon, California

In 1974 my father-in-law, Bill, had purchased a 55 foot trawler. The family was going to cruise for at least a year down to South America. He had asked me to accompany him along with my mother-in-law, Nora; brother-in-law, Gary; and a friend, Eddy, to move the "Tapatia" up from San Diego to my home on the estuary in Alameda. The estuary was a deep water channel dividing Alameda from Oakland, California. We would be fitting the boat with the latest in smoke alarms and a Haylon Fire Suppression System. I had made a shift trade at work and took six days off, which should have been plenty of time to get the boat north. The day before our trip, I flew to San Diego to fuel and prepare for an early departure. With 2500 gallons of diesel aboard, food, and a last minute equipment check done, it was early to bed.

164

Too much pizza and not enough sleep greeted the morning. Five a.m., and we were on our way. By 6:00 a.m., we were pointed north, ten miles out to sea west of La Jolla, and into the rollers. I was at the wheel and feeling pretty good that I wasn't seasick. The wheelhouse doors and windows were closed to keep out the fog and cold. Bill was at the radar; it didn't seem to be working, which was not good considering the weather and shipping lanes. Seven a.m., I was starting to get drowsy when it hit me... out the door, down to the back of the boat... you might have guessed it, sea sick to the max. All I could do for the next 10 hours was crawl from the railing to lay flat on my back on the deck, frying in the afternoon sun.

By 6:00 p.m., Gary called out to his severely sunburned brother-in-law, "Look, Dave, Avalon Harbor, and Catalina Island!"

I thought to myself, *maybe if I crawl to the front of the boat I will arrive sooner and can get off on solid ground,* as if 55 feet would make any difference. They tied the boat to a buoy in the anchorage and helped me onto our rowboat. I've never known how good a beach could feel. I laid there until dark when the family insisted I must move or be carried away by high tide. *Do I care?*

The next day we moved north a couple of miles to White's Landing and stayed the night. My mother-in-law thought I was starting to get some color back, but then, upon closer examination, saw that the color was just sunburn. Below the sunburned red, I was still pea green. Day three, we crossed to the mainland and stayed the night in Ventura Harbor. It was the Fourth of July and we had the best seats in town below the fireworks. Day four, passing Santa Barbara while moving through the oil platforms, we counted close to 100 blue sharks sunning themselves near the surface. We were three miles off the beach and could see both the surfers and the sharks. Hmm, no fear! We continued north to Point Conception anchorage for the night, where we rescued a girl in a rowboat caught on the outgoing tide. That night we had 40 mile an hour winds at anchor, with not much sleep.

Day five began with a 5:00 a.m. departure into a bank of fog. I stayed on the bow for two purposes, fresh air and to watch for ships that would have loved to make us into flotsam and jetsam, as if I could see a thing. Fog will play tricks on you; there is no clue as to how far ahead you are seeing until, out of the void, a sail appears about 500 yards ahead. Perspective! I then realized that, if I see a freighter, I'll have time to say "s@# happens," and then be drowned. Three p.m., Bill found San Simeon Harbor by navigating with the depth finder only, quite a feat. By this time I knew that I'd rather be lost in the middle of a full blown factory fire than at sea, but there was no turning back at this point. I wasn't a Christian yet but I was learning a great lesson: sometimes, even I need help.

A day of rest at Hearst Castle anchorage followed by a 5:00 a.m. departure north. By 8:00 a.m. in the heavy seas from a hurricane out of Mexico, and the smell of smoke. *Great... seasick and smoke ...this is not good.* I climbed to the wheelhouse to smell burning electrical wiring. After investigating all compartments, the odor must have been coming from below.

My brother-in-law yelled from the starboard side of the main deck, "There's fire in the engine room!"

I descended the ladder to the main salon, and out the side door, to see Gary standing in black smoke with a look of: *Well, do something! You're the firefighter!*

I think, *Me? Let's see... Oh I know; I'll throw up.*

166

Then I remembered the 100 blue sharks we counted a couple of days ago sunning off Santa Barbara and waiting for lunch. I decided to stay aboard. Leaning headfirst down into smoke pouring from the engine room, I tried to see the fire. *No good,* so I backed down the stairs to the deck expecting to feel my feet burning at any moment. On hands and knees, I could see forward to the main electrical panel which was in flames and burning up against one of the fuel tanks which we had filled four days earlier with 2500 gallons of diesel. This motivated me even more. Gary handed me a dry chemical extinguisher which I planned to discharge in short blasts. Due to the salt air corrosion, it stuck open and emptied its full contents in one long burst. Now I was trying to breathe smoke and talcum powder, which was not really conducive to good air exchange.

I climbed to fresh air, hung over the rail, asked God if I was dying, took another breath, and descended again with a CO2 extinguisher. One hour later we were reduced to using buckets of water. The engines had shut down and we are rolling in the trough, totally on our side. In my sick, foggy mind I heard my father-in-law on the radio speaking to someone who I thought was the Coast Guard. The man heard our "Mayday" but had very broken English and I thought, *why the heck do we have someone on the emergency channel that can't speak English?*

Bill came out of the wheel house, looked down at what was left of Gary, Eddie, and me, and said what he thought was an encouraging word. "Dave, look!"

What I saw was a freighter steaming dead on us and thought, *we got the fire out, the contents of my stomach is out, the smoke in my lungs is almost out and now I am going to be crushed by a ship. Are we having fun yet?* But, in fact, the cargo ship out of

167

I Could Have Died A Thousand Deaths

Amsterdam had heard our "Mayday" and was about to turn and stop upwind to block the waves; it really helped.

One more chore to do; I must go below into my stateroom which was on the other side of the bulkhead near the fire. I was worried that there could still be fire in the wall. I have to admit at this point, I just wanted to sit down and quit, but then the thought of the sharks came to mind, and I picked up an axe and proceeded to chop holes in father-in-law's beautiful boat. The fire was out and overhead we heard the roar of a C-130 at about 50 feet, parachuting a canister of extinguishers which promptly drifted away and down 50 fathoms below. An hour later the Coast Guard helicopter out of Monterey was hovering overhead and dropping extinguishers by cable to the forward deck. What a trip to watch pros at work. I was on the receiving end for a change and have much admiration for their professionalism.

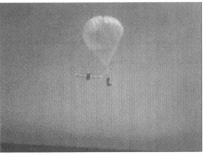

Five hours later, an 83 foot cutter, the Cape Hedge from Morro Bay, arrived and threw us a tow line. Another five terrifying hours under tow in following seas thinking we might capsize and drown at any moment. My father-in-law, Bill, was doing a heroic job of keeping us from capsizing with Nora standing at his side to encourage. About 3:00 p.m., I found myself wedged into the back railing holding onto our Zodiac raft thinking, *when we capsize I'll have the raft and be able to pick up the other four as they break the surface. My girls are up from their naps screaming with delight, the fireman are sitting at the kitchen table talking and drinking coffee, and I'm going to die.* Feeling helpless, *I must need God.*

As I looked toward the coastline ten miles away, I could just make out Hearst Castle on the hill shining in the sun; it seemed to be six inches high with some ant-like cars passing on Highway 1. I had driven that road many times, and wondered what it would be like to be on a boat. Now I knew. Sitting backward on the stern did two things: it gave me time to think and time to watch for every eleventh wave to roll us on our side. When that happened, I would prepare to jump. Thanks to the 2500 gallons of fuel low in the hull, we stayed upright and arrived safely but unnerved in Morro Bay. After tying up to the pier, we all wanted to get to solid ground so off we went to a restaurant.

Morro Bay

At the table with no appetite, we started to relive the last 12 hours. As we talked, I began to realize that the numbness was lifting and the feeling in my body had begun returning. With that, I noticed that my pants were still wet and my shoes and socks were soaked. We laughed and returned to a semi-quiet night in a motel trusting that the mooring lines would hold the boat. The next morning the Coast Guard Captain paid us a visit. We thought that was really considerate of him. As we sat and talked, it became apparent that something was bothering him. Finally he came clean.

This is his story of the event: "You know, our main job here is to respond to old fishing boats that should not be floating, let alone fishing, 20 miles off the coast. We get calls over and over again, and have to drag the same boats in. It's frustrating. So, yesterday morning at home while eating my breakfast, I get this call from the officer on duty that a boat is in distress and needs a tow. Thinking it's one of my regulars, I return to my breakfast, then take a leisurely stroll in the morning sun to the wharf."

"I see that my lieutenant is running down the dock yelling, 'Where have you been? Didn't you hear we have the trawler, Tapatia, on fire off of Point San Martin?' I asked, 'What do you mean?' He replied, 'The cutter is ready to get underway.' Now I'm running and holding my breath. We may be five hours away in heavy seas because of the hurricane from Mexico. *I've really blown it,* I thought. 'Cast off!' the captain continues. We got underway as I stepped onboard and broke all speed records getting to you. Most of my crew was sea sick but we didn't slow until we saw that you were still afloat. I'm so grateful you are safe and just had to get this off of my chest."

We all laughed and knew that we had beaten the odds. The Coast Guard crew had done a great job of rescuing us and confession was good for the soul.

I returned home to work. Three weeks and $25,000 in repairs later, the Tapatia arrived in my backyard. We set about patching, repainting and, fitting the boat with the best firefighting system ever built. The in-laws did sail for two years in the Sea of Cortez with no major mishaps. As for me, I'll stay on dry ground and fight fires that I can walk around.

The Saga Continues

Coast Guard Cutter, The Cape Hedge

In 1988, the Alameda Fire Department fireboat was to participate with the surrounding waterfront cities to organize mutual aid. We met at Oakland's fireboat pier in Jack London Square and spent the afternoon planning, talking and eating. We compared each other's boats, sure that ours was the best.

Inspecting the different vessels, I climbed aboard the 83 foot Navy ship, by far the largest of our group. Alameda had one of the smallest boats in the fleet but we were fast and efficient. To my surprise the Navy's 83 foot cutter also participated. I marveled at its size and commented to the skipper that this ship reminded me of a Coast Guard cutter, the Cape Hedge, which rescued my boat in Morro Bay in 1973.

To my complete shock, the captain said, "This <u>was</u> the Cape Hedge. It had been transferred to the Navy a couple of years back, repainted from white to gray, to cover San Francisco Bay. You're standing on your rescue ship." *Wow!*

How Does an Alameda Fireman and his Pastor get Stoned by Hamas?

October 1, 1989 - Bound for an Israeli Adventure

Our church had received a new pastor earlier. Larry and I soon realized we had much in common, a love of Israel and history. Larry heard that I had traveled to the land in 1979 and came back with an overwhelming love of biblical and ancient Jewish history.

As we talked, it became apparent that we were on the same page, which generated a question. "Dave, do you think you could guide me in Israel? I would rather team up with you than a tour group."

"Sounds like a plan," I replied. "Let's go on the Feast of Tabernacles, in early October, when the land is teeming with life."

We booked on El Al Airlines for security reasons, and found ourselves on an 18-hour flight to Tel Aviv. Upon arrival, we spent one night in the Hilton, and then went on to Jerusalem in our Subaru (think sardine can car). Approaching Jerusalem, I wanted Larry's first view of the Old City to be from the Mount of Olives overlook. We circled north of the city, east through the Kidron Valley, and up the mount on a one-lane road. Near the top, we turned south through a small Palestinian village to the overlook.

Knowing that we were more than two years into the intifada (*awakening, uprising*), I was mindful of the danger. Before us were military Jeeps and empty streets, so I felt safe. At the overlook, taking in the panorama of Jerusalem, Larry was thrilled. The Bible was coming alive. As he surveyed the view, I was aware of a group of Palestinian teenage boys approaching to sell souvenirs. They quickly became a little too aggressive. "Larry, it's time to go."

As we got into the car, the boys scrambled to get in the back seat. Larry pushed them out and closed the door just as two men with a camel approached. The one man with the camel stopped in front of our car, the other walked up to my window and threatened, "This is our land; you're here now but you won't be for long," which gave me chills.

I quickly reversed the car, backed away, and left. I would have burned rubber if our Subaru had had the power. Remembering a hotel just up the road, I thought we should go there for safety. As we pulled into the parking lot, a group of Arab men moved toward us. Throwing it into reverse and back onto the street, we headed toward the village. Ahead, we saw that the streets were full of

people. What we didn't know was the Palestinians had called for a protest strike to start at noon. It was close to one p.m.; the protest was in full swing. The street had gone from empty to crowds overflowing sidewalks.

Holding my breath, not wanting to alarm Larry, I decided I would not stop for any reason. If the crowd tried to stop us, I would run over them. Racing through the streets, the people seemed unconcerned with the Subaru and its neon rental license plates, a telltale sign of foreigners. I made a quick left turn as we were starting our descent into the Kidron Valley with a sigh of relief.

A bottle crashed against the rear window. The cracking of glass brought my attention to the rear view mirror. I gasped as I realized the Arab crowd was suddenly chasing after us. I turned back to see down the hill. A block ahead of us were four Arab men, two on either side of this one-lane road. We had no choice but to accelerate and hope we could escape. The men had each picked up **head size** rocks and seemed to be waiting for us to pass. The first rock was thrown from my side at the hood, the second entered the car through the right rear window in a shower of glass. The third was to come from the right front. The look in the man's eyes is etched in my memory forever.

"Larry, duck!"

Too late. This rock entered through the right passenger window striking Larry on the right side of his face. I heard Larry groan as we drove to freedom. Looking in the rear view mirror, I could see Larry's face with a large gash; blood was already flowing onto his lap.

"Larry, can you hear me?"

"Yes."

"Stay with me! I'll get help."

Now as I ascended toward Jerusalem, I saw a fire station. Relieved, I thought, *great! We'll get help here.* I knocked on the door, but it was vacant. Back in the car, feeling like the city might be trying to kill us, I continued up the hill knowing that, when we topped the Valley Road, we would be in East Jerusalem. This is the Arab section. I decided again that I wouldn't stop until I saw Israeli soldiers or police.

"Larry, are you still with me?"

"Yeah," came a muffled reply.

There was now blood on the seat, and his lap was covered, along with broken eyeglasses, and shards of auto glass. Knowing that we could encounter more rioters as we topped the hill, I again got ready to barrel through. Relief, as I discovered we were on a four-lane divided boulevard, with light traffic. Two blocks down the road, I saw an Israeli personnel carrier approaching. I thought, *I'll flag him down.* At that moment they started to turn left in front of me. All I could think to do was speed up and cut them off. As I did, their response while skidding to a stop, was to exit the vehicle with weapons drawn, thinking I may be a bomber or some other nut.

As Larry and I exited the car with our hands up, I yelled, "Terrorist attack!"

When they saw my hands up, Larry covered with blood, and no windshield in our car, they realized what was happening. The soldiers sat Larry down and began to bandage his wounds as I tried

I Could Have Died A Thousand Deaths

to communicate with Israelis that only spoke Hebrew.

I heard Larry say, "Oh, I hope this doesn't make U.S. news before I can speak to Becky," but it did.

In my shock, I hadn't realized that a newsreel camera was in my face. The cameraman must have been in the van with the soldiers. One half-hour later, I found myself standing in a Jerusalem intersection, talking to Israeli soldiers, and waving good-bye to my friend in the afternoon sun as the ambulance transported him to Hadassah Hospital. And for me, I was off to the police station. Larry had wanted excitement, but not quite this much!

Five p.m. - Still sitting in the police station, seemingly forgotten, I realized, *the only way I am going to get out of here is to say I need to go to the hospital.* So that's what I did, and they let me go. Taking a taxi ride, I entered Hadassah Emergency. The nurses brought me to Larry who was still in shock but, by now had been stitched, bandaged, hydrated, and was being cared for by a 30 year old man that spoke English. *Thank you, Lord,* I prayed silently. The man, who I thought was an orderly, turned out to be the head of Neurosurgery. Because of the nature of the attack, and we being Americans, the hospital had given us their best care.

Eleven p.m. - I had just left Larry in good hands and was off to our hotel and some rest. Finally collapsing on the bed, the adrenalin was keeping me awake so I turned on the television. In the 1990's there were no English speaking channels but, being a man, I continued to channel check anyway. I came to what seemed to be the news. On the screen, to my horror, appeared an Israeli intersection, a personnel carrier, a car with no windows, and then a full screen shot of my face and Larry being bandaged. I thought, *Oh no, now everyone in Israel will know my face. Home sounds really good right now.*

But we were 8,000 miles away and being guarded by the Israeli Government. Larry was kept another day in the hospital, and I sat in the local mall people watching while sipping coffee. To my surprise, folks seemed to be watching me; it was a little unnerving to see total strangers take a second look, and I was sure that they knew who I was.

Day Four - Larry was released, and we were assigned a bodyguard and an archeologist to take us anywhere we wanted to go. The doors had opened to Jerusalem's underground and, thanks to our mishap, we were treated well.

Day Seven - Shabbat starts at dusk. We decided to walk to the Western Wall and watch the worshipers begin their Sabbath celebration. Returning to our hotel by a shorter route, through the Old City to Jaffa Gate, seemed best; it would take less time. By now, you would think we would have wised up. Everyone in town knew my face, and Larry had a giant bandage on his, covering a fractured jaw, forty stiches, and a crushed cheekbone. As we passed the Israeli guard into the Old City, we turned left and headed for home. The streets were narrow and empty, the shadows making everything darker. Larry and I were both thinking to ourselves that this was not a great idea. Just at that moment, we heard a voice out of the darkness ask, "Are you men Americans?"

Those chills again returned to my spine. In one fluid movement, we reversed direction and headed back as fast as our legs could carry us, praying that we would see that guard again before our heads were removed. We did, and again breathed a sigh of relief. Returning to our hotel the safer way, I thought to myself, *we're not in Kansas anymore, Dorothy!*

Day Eight - In our hotel, the Jewish workers were off for Sabbath. That meant the help were all Palestinians. *Now that was calming.*

I Could Have Died A Thousand Deaths

We were approached by two Arab men that wanted to talk.

We passed pleasantries and they finally got to their point. "You know, we are aware of who you are, and want you to realize that your stoning was not personal. It's just that you are Americans and are on the side of the Israelis."

I replied, "Thanks," while silently thinking, *that make us feel a whole lot better. What's a few scars between friends?*

Prior to our trip, a friend of mine in the States, Dr. Nancy Del Grande, a nuclear physicist, had developed an infrared sensory device that could see variations in structure five feet below ground level. I had helped her do the test run at Mission Santa Cruz, an archeology site, five years earlier. Nancy had asked me, "Dave, could you take this video of the test to a friend of mine in Israel?"

I, of course, responded, "Sure."

So I hand-carried a video tape from Lawrence Livermore Lab to the archeologist for review as he was going to try to find the foundation of Herod's Temple on the mount. I was interrogated for 45 minutes by three different Israeli airport officials and almost didn't make the flight to Israel. Because Lawrence Livermore Laboratory is a nuclear facility, the video sent up tons of red flags. *Am I having fun yet?*

After ten days of excruciating experiences, we were invited to the home of Nancy's friends, Stanley and Helen Goldfoot, back on the Mount of Olives. The view of the Temple at night, across the valley, was breathtaking. We were sitting at dinner at the table of an Israeli militant, who had helped Menachem Begin blow up the King David Hotel in 1947. There we were: Larry, with that huge bandage on his face; me, a television star with a video tape the

Israeli Government might question; another guest Tuvia Sagiv, an archaeologist, who had just been released that day from prison for bombing an Arab location; and a beautiful woman, all at dinner on the Mount of Olives. It could have been the scene from a poorly written mystery novel.

As you can imagine, Larry and I mostly just listened that night, and were amazed at the stories, thinking the Mossad might crash through the door at any moment.

Twenty-Four Years Future, 2014

Since leaving the Bay Area in 1996, I had lost contact with Nancy until two months ago when I called and found her still trying to get the Israeli Government to approve a flyover. Her machine had been improved upon and used by the Israeli military to overfly the Philadelphi Corridor between Gaza and the Egyptian border to find Hamas' smuggling tunnels, with good success. This is to show you that people all over the world are working to restore Israel and, in God's timing, it will happen. Only He knows when. We are to keep looking up, knowing that He is in charge and the work will be completed.

Headed for Home - Who Said I'm a Doctor?

By the time we left Israel for home, we were quite exhausted but filled to overflowing with life experiences and firsthand information from the epicenter of the world. The night we flew out of Israel, 13 Palestinians were killed at the Temple Mount for dropping rocks from 50 feet onto the worshipers standing below. In the news, it will be reported as the cruel Israelis are at it again, killing

I Could Have Died A Thousand Deaths

the poor Arabs for dropping a few small pebbles as a nuisance. We know the truth: large slabs of stone from a great height onto a crowded plaza below, and the intifada shifted into second gear.

At 30,000 feet, high over the USA, I felt we were going to make it home, and I could return to the easy life of crawling out of burning buildings and rescuing cats from trees. What could possibly go wrong now? My mistake.

A call came over the intercom, "Is there a doctor onboard?"

No reply, as I got a poke in the ribs from Larry with, "You're a medical guy!"

"No, I'm only an EMT (Emergency Medical Technician)! I'm sleeping and want to go home."

The call came in again, and Larry said to the flight attendant, "Here's your man."

The flight attendant directed, "Come with me. A man in First Class might be having a heart attack and is about to pass out."

"What can I do? I don't have a blood pressure cuff or any first aid equipment." As I approached, the man was blue but breathing. I checked his pulse and tried to calm him. He seemed a little better.

The copilot asked, "How is he?"

I responded, "I need a blood pressure cuff."

He replied, "The only one we have is locked in the cockpit and only a doctor can open the medical box."

I said, "I need it to do anything more."

He responded, "Come with me."

I now found myself sitting in the cockpit of a 767 talking to the pilot, who said, "I'll open the box. Dave, should we land in Nebraska? It's up to you."

"Me?" I thought, *I want to go home!* "Let me check him."

The man had calmed down, his blood pressure was within limits, and he seemed to be resting comfortably, so I gave orders to fly on. *What power!*

Again back in my seat, Larry smiled. One hour later, the flight attendant approached me again. *What now?*

"Dave, we have an older woman who thinks she's going to faint."

I took her blood pressure, whispered sweet nothings in her ear, and reassured her, "Everything is going to be alright."

Once again, back to my seat, with a frown at Larry. He smiled.

An hour later, nearing Nevada, and dozing, "Dave, wake up! Dave! It's me, the flight attendant again. We have a pregnant woman in her ninth month who is very light-headed."

"Okay." But, about this time, thinking *I should get a free airline ticket somewhere,* I was getting the hang of this blood pressure cuff. So I calmed her, assuring her that I would be here if she needed me, *though delivery is far from my favorite maneuver.*

She happened to be in First Class, so I said to the attendant, "I'd better stay up here close to the expectant mother," thinking *I'll just relax in First Class. Let Larry stay comfortably in coach. Aaaah, revenge!*

I Could Have Died A Thousand Deaths

I never thought I would love LAX, but it was paradise compared to where we had been the last week and a half.

What have I learned in the 25 years since this nightmare? I love the land and the people of Israel. Patty and I have traveled there twice more without incident. Why? Because we go with savvy guides. We say now that, "If you are able to get safely out of LAX, there won't be any problems." And, finally, "If you really want to understand the dynamics of the Middle East, you must go, you must study their history and, above all, do not listen to politicians or talking heads that haven't a clue about what's really happening."

<u>There is Hope After All</u>

I had been pondering the future generations for years, when I was approached in a grocery store in Redding, California. I was in the produce aisle when I felt a tap on my back at about waist high. I turned to look. Not seeing anyone my size, I noticed a young boy, maybe six years old, looking up at me.

This brave young man had walked up to a large, gruff, older man and asked, "Are you a veteran?" He and his mom had seen my T-shirt which reads, "Freedom Congress In Support of Our Troops."

I replied, "Yes, I am."

The boy, looking up and straight into my eyes, extended his hand to shake mine and said, "Thank you."

I was blown away… me, without words. All I could say was, "Thank you!" as I looked at him and then his proud mother across the room observing her son.

There was no I-phone, no Game Boy to be seen, no Harry Potter pictures on his shirt, no toy cars in his hand, just he and I face-to-face, hand-to-hand. I think I smiled and turned, dumbfounded, to go on shopping. I didn't know what else to say.

As I moved through the store, I couldn't get this young boy and his mom out of my mind. I needed to talk to them again to tell his mother what hope he had restored in me, hope that there is a remnant in this generation today just as there has always been, a remnant that gets it. There are still people in this world that will take their place on the battlefield of the Twin Towers of today and tomorrow for their love of God and country. I later found them checking out and waited to speak to his mom. I approached again and thanked them, telling of my fire and military career and how much his hand and words meant to me. I then shared my amazement at her son and commended her parenting skills.

She said, "His dad is in the army in Pakistan."

I replied that I would be praying for him.

She smiled and then said, "That gives me goose bumps."

As they walked out the door, I felt that I needed to do more for them. But they are gone and I may never see them again. It's been three days and I still cannot forget this young boy. It really is simple, parents; put your busywork aside and talk to your sons. They so need their moms and dads. They don't need things; they need you. I know this young boy is on his way, and I pray that I'll see him again. *Lord, please protect his father.* Men, it's time to step up and be counted. I know this young boy will. Ability is in all of us; it only needs to be activated. Just do it!

I Could Have Died A Thousand Deaths

When an Israeli soldier is through with his training, he climbs Masada in the Negev Desert to receive his rifle and a Bible. The rifle is to defend his country and the Bible is to tell him the reason why he must defend it. Without an understanding of history, he cannot understand the future.

Masada
(Mits-a-da)

The Sinai Desert Near the Dead Sea

Their training starts years before the military, in grammar school. Children, as part of their schooling, take field trips to all the borders of their land. By the time of graduation they have explored Israel from one end to the other. They have been taught the history of the land and now they must defend it. Thus at Masada, their final hurdle, they're ready.

184

The battle for Masada was the last struggle for sovereignty of the land in Jewish history until the return of the people from exile and reestablishment of a nation in 1948. The Zealots on Masada in 73 AD were waiting to be slaughtered by Roman forces. They buried a piece of the scroll of Ezekiel 37, describing the dry bones coming to life again, the hope in their future that God would restore the nation. Two thousand years future, in 1964, Yigael Yadin, an archeologist who fought in the War of Independence for a *"land born in one day,"* discovered this text. Nine years future of that, during the 1973 feast of Yom Kippur, when Egypt swept down on an unsuspecting Israel at prayer and holiday, a commando unit being overrun in the Sinai Desert was surrounded and asked for permission to retreat.

The commander said no, "Masada shall not fall again."

This meant, if you give up here, your families will die at home in Jerusalem and Tel Aviv like our people on Masada did two millennia ago. That's how the whole spirit of Masada emerged. There's only one chapter in the Bible that describes the resurrection and return of a nation to its homeland, Ezekiel 37.

In 1964, Yigael Yadin was excavating Masada. As he worked in the synagogue ruin, with shrieks of joy, he found a piece of parchment from a scroll of Ezekiel Chapter 37 buried in the floor. After almost 2000 years, where the bones had last bleached in the sun, a message from God was found. Dry bones…arise and walk; you're home and alive again.

The story of Masada is told by the first century historian, Josephus in "Wars of the Jews," Book VII, Chapter VIII, and verse 6.

Masada has become a place of pilgrimage for Israelis. Since the Diaspora and Holocaust, the people return here to remember and say there is no other option for us; this is it, we have no other place to go. The world doesn't want us so we must fight to stay where God has chosen to plant us since time immemorial. So, "Masada shall not fall again."

The military has since adopted Masada as a place of initiation and dedication. They come here after finishing basic training to march 1300 feet up the snake path, a very tiring journey. They take stretchers and carry soldiers to the summit, the same trail that was used to carry King Herod to his palace. When the Israeli soldiers get to the top, they receive two gifts from their commander: **a rifle and a Bible.** The rifle is to defend their country and the Bible is to know why, because there is no future if you don't understand your past. - *My people are destroyed for lack of knowledge. (Hosea 4:6)*

In their oath, they say Masada shall not fall again. This should also be a reminder to America. Anyone who doesn't know that the

United States was founded on Judeo-Christian principles is living in a dream world. Every soldier was given a Bible in World War II. If you don't know your past, you will not understand the future. We in America must get back to God's Word, for unless we know where we have come from, we won't know where we are going.

We, as a nation, are connected by blood (the Blood of the Lamb) to Israel. Unless we understand as a nation who we are spiritually, as well as physically, we are severed, cut off from our root, the (olive tree) patriarchs, prophets, Psalms, and Gospels, which will cause us to shrivel and die. We are contributing to our own demise and allowing destruction that isn't in God's plan. When Jesus, Peter, Paul, Mathew, Mark, Luke, and John were quoting Scripture, there was no New Testament; they were quoting the Old Testament, the Scriptures. They went back to the Torah, the prophets and writings, not knowing that someday their words would be compiled into 27 books called the New Testament, which, simply put, are God's commentary on the Old Testament.

We must understand that, as believers, we also have to know where we have come from in order to know where we are going. If you get your information from CNN or talk radio day by day, you're being led by the talking heads, which are being led by ratings, which are being led by their agenda. How do you know truth? We must know our history to verify the opinion of others. People love prophecy teaching because it deals with where we are going but, if you lose sight of where you have been, your history, your legacy, you will be confused about who you are and where you are going. There is only one way to be sure, and that is God's Word with God's Spirit.

Military Bible - WW II

Jerusalem 2008
Burtons and Franks

Syria Lebanon Border

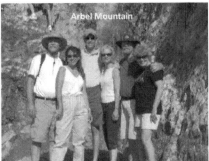

Arbel Mountain

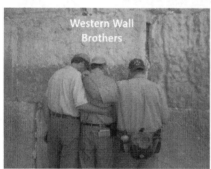

Western Wall
Brothers

Bob & Susan Black
Top of Arbel Mt.

Dead Sea

PART FIVE

The Christian Years

In 1977 I became a Christian and, armed with this understanding, God has helped me put perspective on what we firefighters do, how to look and value the life He has given me. The next three chapters are what I have learned. God has been there all my life, even when I didn't know it; and, if asked, He will be there for you also.

God Spoke to Me This Morning - January 18, 2004

My pastor taught last night about the burning bush found in Exodus 3 and Mark 12:26. For the first time I understood why, on my last shift in the Alameda Fire Department, and the last fire run of my career, was a response to a **burning bush** fire. Yes, really. A "burning bush" is the way the call came in. God was calling me aside to tell me, "Well done. Leave the fire department behind, find Patty and go in a new direction." He made it clear that He will take care of Erin, Bree, and Macee.

"Go to a large place and share what I, the Lord, am giving you. Share your land, your home, your gifts, and your understanding of Israel. I placed you in a Jewish family for a reason; don't ever forget it. Having done all, stand your ground. Make no apologies!"

So, having found Patty, (in all actuality, God had brought her into my house), I loved and prayed for Erin, Bree and Macee. Then Patty and I headed for a new life in Redding. A three-way miracle trade of homes secured our finances. The home God sent us to has been the home base of our life until the last several months. We adventured, explored, worked in four churches, shared Passover with more than 600 friends over the years, met and became friends with Bob and Susan Black, joined the Messianic movement, and

190

traveled to Israel twice. On the second trip, we brought four friends with us, Dave and Phyllis, and Richard and Kathryn. We have shared God's backyard with hundreds of children, our church family, and have known 50 Simpson University kids thanks to Michelle and Jason. Then, ten years later, another hundred or so Simpson students came into our lives. We have taught every chance we get about Israel, the Jews, and God's plan revealed in His Word, the Bible. We have ministered to our neighbors; and have watched our redwood tree (which represented our ministry) grow beyond all expectations. When I had the feeling that our patio slab should be built upon, the Lord sent a wonderful friend, Craig, to frame the apartment addition which made a safe place for Patty's mom until her home going 3-1/2 years later. The apartment has been used since for meetings, teaching, guests, and family. Why did we do this? Because it's fun to discover God's will for our lives, and to know He has much more in store for us.

"For I know the plans I have for you," declares the LORD, "plans to prosper you and not to harm you, plans to give you hope and a future." (Jeremiah 29:11-12)

***Light and Dark, Heat and Cold, Trials and Testing
Have been my teacher through the years.
Continuing on, I will share my first-hand observations***

The Furnace
(Or Tested by Fire)

My Destiny – 1959

At age 18 I graduated from high school with no interest in college and not knowing what was coming next. I was offered a furnace tender's job in an aluminum and brass foundry. I said yes and

191

began a journey that is still in process. The foundry, melting metal, heat and fire, have spoken to me many times since. God was setting me up for great life lessons, which I'm still learning today.

*The words of the LORD are pure; as silver tried in **a furnace** on the earth,* **(Psalm 12:6)**

*The **crucible** for silver and the **furnace** for gold,* **(Proverbs 27:21)**

*In this you greatly rejoice, even though now for a little while, if necessary, you have been put through **various trials**, that the proof of your faith, being more precious than gold which is perishable, even though **tested by fire**, may be found to result in praise and glory and honor at the revelation of Jesus Christ;* **(1 Peter 1:5-7)**

Seven a.m.

The steps of the foundry-man echo as he strides the length of the cool, dark cavern. The master furnace tender lights the gas-fired burners as the molders take their places behind the large piles of black sand and clay a safe distance away from the heat. From this

At age 18 I graduated from high school

position they will prepare the sand molds to receive molten metal. Light fills the far end of the cavern as blowers introduce air pressure into the gas. The air encircles the crucible in its chamber with a tornado-like roar. Flames appear from the top and side openings of the furnace.

Now the tender must use caution. Quickly the room warms until outside doors and overhead vents cannot keep pace with the rise of temperature. As the heat increases, the tender (that would be *me)* drops the first ingot of brass into the crucible; quickly he steps back, a smell of singed hair fills his nostrils. The master tender looks down with a chuckle; he sees the hair of his forearm curled and charred. Droplets of sweat appear on his forehead as the temperatures rise and the brass starts to melt. Knowing that the next ingots must be warmed to remove the moisture before being dropped into the molten metal, he approaches the furnace ever so carefully and sets them on the top edge. The tools are heated and ready.

Now is the time to add more ingots to the furnace. By now his clothes are soaked with sweat. He approaches the furnace with gloved hands, and lifts the outside edge of the two-foot ingot to slip it down into the furnace. As cold hits hot, the metal spits, pops and sputters. The tender quickly steps back but droplets of brass shoot out and burn through his shirt. He has learned that, when hit by the metal projectiles, he can lean forward and they will burn right through his shirt to drop harmlessly on the floor. The tender knows that burns are not nearly as bad as the **fear** of the burns. The process continues five, maybe six more ingots, all the time the metal seems to be **attacking** for it doesn't want to change. The master furnace tender knows its final outcome and is willing to **turn up the heat** to gain perfect results.

Consider it all joy, my brethren, when you encounter various *trials, knowing that the **testing of your metal** (faith) produces endurance. **(James 1:2)***

The thermometer is dipped into the liquefied brass many times as the tender waits tolerantly knowing that only **heat, time, and patience** will gain the perfect result. **2350 degrees** Fahrenheit... the time has come. On the floor near the furnace is a pouring shank. The shank is a circle of iron with a straight bar on one side and a straight bar with a T handle on the other. The lid of the furnace is swung to one side. Flames leap high as the tender and his helper set tongues over the crucible. With one quick lifting motion the 300 pound crucible is removed from the furnace and set in the shank. The master tender then takes a skimmer and removes slag floating on its top. Slag consists of the impurities that have come to the surface during the heating process. He knows by the reflection of his face in the molten reddish orange mirror that it's almost ready.

*Moreover, he made the laver of **brass** with its base of bronze, from the **melted** mirrors of the serving women who served at the doorway of the tent of meeting. **(Exodus 38:8)***

Now comes the most critical procedure, a long ceramic tube with hose attached to a tank of **chlorine gas,** is forced down into the bottom of the crucible and turned on. Escaping gas causes the metal again to agitate. The metal rolls, bubbles and spits at anything or anyone within range. It **resists** the change that's coming with all its fury. This procedure removes any **deep-seated** impurities (**sins**) that are not apparent on the surface.

*God sees not as man sees, for **man looks at the surface**, but the Master [LORD] **looks deeper** [at the heart]. **(I Samuel 16:7)***

A final quick skim, a dip with the thermometer, and a glance at His reflection. **It's ready!** The master foundry-man and helper (*disciple*) lift the shank and begin the pour. As the metal is released, it flows wherever the master directs it. Everywhere it goes it flows easily and is shaped into whatever mold the master chooses. **It's malleable, hot and pliable. It's creating new things, solid, pure and perfect things. The resistance is gone.**

*For who resists His will? On the contrary, who are you, O man, who answers back to God? Does the thing **molded** say to the **molder**, "Why did you make me like this?" (**Romans 9:19-21**)*

The outcome is exactly what the brass was intended for, but without **time, heat, and patience,** the metal would still be a cold, hard, block of brass, on a pallet in the rain and weather, waiting, as people pass by wondering, *What on earth are those ingots for? Do*

they (I) have any earthly or, for that matter, heavenly use?

New sounds are introduced into the foundry: air hammers, forklifts, grinders, and happy shouts from men kidding each other.

"Hey Joe! What do you think of Davey boy, our new tender? Will he last?"

"Nah, he's too good looking. If he does, it'll take years for him to master his craft," he replies with laugh.

I Could Have Died A Thousand Deaths

Men, seasoned men, strong men, and me, an awkward 18 year old just out of high school trying to prove my worth in this masculine fraternity. I must gain acceptance from these craftsmen by hard work and a listening ear. Babe, the foreman, had carefully taught me the ropes on that first day. He had all the answers. He was a man of five foot eight inches who seemed to tower over me with a tight black welder's hat, a day-old beard, and a one-inch cigar in the left corner of his mouth. I watched that cigar for two years; it never grew or shrunk. I learned quickly that what he said was not repeated but was **truth**. The look in his eyes told me that this is serious business; we don't play around here. I was expected to listen and respond. **Yes sir!**

Six months later I would learn that what he said had great purpose. Nine a.m., first pour of the day. This day it's aluminum, the process was similar to the brass but its temperature was much lower, **1250 degrees** Fahrenheit. With great dexterity I light the furnaces, and slide the ingots into the crucible. The temperature is attained, and I move with a newly found confidence as Babe looks on from his office window.

*Behold, the **eye** of the **LORD** (Babe) is on those who fear Him.*
(Psalm 33:18)

I feel his watchful eye and think, ***"I am good!"*** In my hurry to prove myself, I had forgotten the foundry-man's golden rule, to preheat all tools that sit overnight on the floor as they absorb moisture, which doesn't mix with molten metal. We lift the crucible of aluminum to the shank; I grab a skimmer from the floor and quickly walk to the molten metal. A confident swipe of the skimmer... I hear an explosion! *What's that? It's me... I'm on fire!* The metal is running down my arms into my gloves. I drop the skimmer and throw off my gloves as the skimmer re-enters the crucible. Another explosion, which empties the rest of the metal. What doesn't stick to my skin blows past me and up 20 feet to burn into the ceiling. I claw at my eyelid and feel the men tearing what remains of my shirt off to brush the metal that has penetrated my arms, side and back. There before me is Babe, his face showing concern. His eyes say, *"Do you get it?"* My expression says, *"Yeah, I get it."* No need for words.

Two hours later I've returned from the hospital. Babe asks, "Ya want to go home?"

"Nah, I'll work." The pain of the burns was subdued by the pain of a lesson well learned.

*How blessed is the man who finds **wisdom**, and the man who gains **understanding**. (Proverbs 3:13)*

Yes, Master, I **understand**. May I use this lesson throughout life; it has now become **wisdom**. I'm beginning to learn what it takes to be a Master.

*See, I have called by name Bezalel, of the tribe of Judah. And I have filled him with the Spirit of God in **wisdom**, in **understanding**, and in **knowledge**, to make artistic designs for work in gold, in silver, and in brass, that he may work in all kinds of **craftsmanship**. (Exodus 31:2-5)*

Jesus came in the flesh to set an example of what it meant to master His craft. He was and is Master (God) but He set aside his Godhead for a season and came to earth. He showed us all that He knew the process. Born into a working class family He learned His craft of masonry and woodworking by patience, obedience, practice and application. He chose this, knowing that He would have to go through the furnace (cross) for us physically and spiritually.

I Could Have Died A Thousand Deaths

He would endure the **fires** of hell and be **poured out** for our transgressions, so that the world would be reshaped and conformed into the likeness of the Master. **(Isaiah 53:12b)**

(Daniel 3:26): Shadrach, Meshach and Abednego had learned this truth when they walked through the furnace and were not burned. We also can walk through the fire and not be burned. The fact is, we will not even have the smell of smoke if we master what trial we have to go through. How do we do this? We consult Jesus, the fourth Person in the furnace, the Master. We hold on to Him, we call out to Him, we listen to Him, and we have patience.

I have learned in my 74 years (40 years as a believer) that God's timing and mine are much different and with a much different purpose. I now realize that the Holy Spirit was there from the beginning, shaping and wooing me through the circumstances of life. If we find ourselves in the furnace, we need to be aware that the Master will never turn up the fire to destroy, but rather to draw the best, the most pure, and most refined out of us, for His purposes.

How blessed is the man whose strength is in Thee; in whose heart are the highways to Zion [**success!**]. ***Passing through*** *the valley of weeping... on the other side are* ***streams of joy.*** *(Psalm 84:5-7)*

The operative word in this passage is **passing through**. God will never leave us nor forsake us. He is **always tending the foundry** with His watchful eye. I lost my dad at age eight. His being a firefighter brought me into close contact with men of character. They looked after my brother and me. My hunger for a father caused me to seek and listen to their wise counsel. The lessons learned in that foundry, six years with Caterpillar Tractor, and 25 years in the fire department, have stood me well. I would probably still be in the foundry if I hadn't listened to Joe, another man of influence, a man of quiet manner, different from the others. But I was learning to look for and hear wisdom.

Two years in the foundry trade, master of my craft, sitting at lunch one day, Joe asked the question, "Dave, why are you still here?"

I said, "Because I feel accepted and am doing a good job."

Joe replied, "Dave, get out of here! The foundry will make you old before your time."

I listened and heard. Two months later, I was gone.

My friends, wisdom is all around us; all we have to do is stop and listen. Listen to the Holy Spirit as you search the Word of God, which is a lamp to your feet, and a light to your path. Listen for the Holy Spirit as you look to people.

*"But the Helper, the Holy Spirit, whom the Father will send in My name, **He** will teach you all things, and bring to your remembrance all that I said to you." (John 14:26)*

I Could Have Died A Thousand Deaths

At some time in your life you should get on your knees in total darkness and try to find your way. Then turn on a small flashlight and understand what God is explaining in His Word. There are 250 references to light and 161 to darkness in the Bible. Maybe there's something to be learned.
Below is what I have learned:

The Holy Spirit Directs My Path
(Or the Light Saber)

Patrick's Point State Park, Northern California, 1974, 5:00 p.m.

Our family is on vacation at Patrick's Point State Park. While in our motor home, my wife is cooking dinner. Baby Bree is sleeping and I, being a dad and a new Christian, sought to teach my older daughter, Erin, a verse from God's Word. **Psalm 119:105** had interested me; *Word* is used 725 times in the Bible and 37 times alone in Psalm 119.

Thy word is a lamp to my feet, and a light to my path. "What do you think that means, Erin?"

We talked about it and I made a feeble attempt to explain to her

 what I didn't yet understand myself. With dinner over and Bree awake, we decided to go to the evening campfire across the park. The trails were overgrown with ferns and redwood trees; we had hiked through them all day with no trouble. It

200

was dusk but still light enough to find our way to the gathering. We hadn't considered how dark the park would be at night. I grabbed a flashlight and we were off to sit with a large group of people around the fire. Our rangers told amazing stories and led us in singing. Near the end of the night, hot cocoa was offered. Erin wanted to stay but baby Bree was fussy.

Laura said, "Let me take Bree back to the motor home. You two stay."

That seemed like a great solution.

"Here," I said, "take the flashlight to guide you. There seems to be plenty of light and people; we'll find our way."

At the end of the evening's activities, all the groups quickly disappeared into the bush. Erin and I found ourselves alone as we left the light of the campfire behind and walked toward the trailhead. Entering the well-marked path, light quickly dimmed and shadows seemed to engulf us the farther we moved into the trees, like walking into the ocean deeper and deeper. I slowed and took Erin by the hand as we were tripping on the roots and rocks, moving ever so carefully forward. We continued on, Erin's hand grasping tighter and tighter until we had to stop. I bent over to pick her up.

As I straightened again, I lost my sense of direction. I looked but my eyes would not focus in the darkness. **I could see nothing**. The overwhelming feeling was of fear, the fear of not knowing, and fear of what was out there, the need to protect my daughter. *What will happen to us?* I thought to myself. I was feeling an increased heart rate, respirations and helplessness.

"Erin, we're okay. God will help us," I said, trying to show faith and comfort to my daughter though I was feeling much the same way she was. Erin was hanging onto my neck tightly and I was looking into nothingness. We stood still for maybe five minutes trying to make our eyes adjust, intently looking for anything that was familiar in the blackness. Finally I saw what seemed to be a pinpoint of light, remembering that the trail had very small, low-to-the-ground, louvered lights positioned just far enough apart to be useless. *Could it be a trail light?* I wasn't sure but it was our only hope. We move toward this light staggering with almost every step. The closer we approached, the bigger the light became until, standing within five feet of the glow, we could see the trees and ferns all around us, though they seemed like the walls of a cave. What a reprieve within that comforting light.

I felt myself breathe a sigh of reassurance and told Erin, "We're going to be okay." In my relief I could see the trail sign directing us on toward the motor home. *I wish we were inside,* but we weren't there quite yet. There were more trail markers to find. No turning back now; we were in the light but darkness was still surrounding us. The second leg of the trail brought the same results... stumbling into the darkness, vision still limited from the trail light now behind us, I picked up my daughter, stopping to look back as the previous marker is disappearing with no new light in view. I must press on in faith that the rangers have done their job and that we would find another marker. This was an attempt at faith, faith in someone I didn't know, and faith that they had done the job they were supposed to do.

Much later in life I would see that God was teaching me a deeper lesson. We need to know in whom we believe and how to find our way through life. We need to read and learn how to maneuver through all the many difficult decisions of life. His Word guides us and helps to keep us on course; it's our compass. The Bible has been provided by God for just that reason. We can become skilled in finding all the answers to life, school, world situations, work and family by using the tool given us by the Creator of the universe. As I finally let go of the trail light behind and looked ahead, it seemed again in my mind's eye that another light was minutely in view. *Yes, it is!*

As we arrived again within that five-foot perimeter of the illuminated tree cave, we breathed a sigh of relief. We could see now, but still had one more leg to go. Moving out again past the trail sign, I was cursing the designer of the lighting system, but there was nothing to do. We had come too far to turn back. *Oh, to be hugging my family within our small Ford sanctuary.* Knowing what was ahead, I lifted Erin and walked into the abyss, stumbling in our journey. Halfway toward the next light we, again, had to let go of the previous illumination and face total darkness. The obligatory stop, prayer, and eyes straining as I searched for hope, maybe a beam, or a flashlight, or a candle, or a campfire *or, or, yes, yes!* There appeared before me the glow of campers in the trees, and voices and laughter, and hope, and family, and peace and safety and, most of all, gratitude to God that we were safe again.

Later that night I awoke with a start. Looking into the darkness of our camper, I felt the great need to turn on a small light for comfort. The brightness didn't wake the girls but God was saying, "My son, see how needy you humans are for My light?"

I was beginning to see how lost I had been until the light of the Holy Spirit offered a helping hand to me: *Again, therefore, Jesus spoke to them, saying, "I am the light of the world; he who follows me shall not walk in the darkness, but shall have the light of life." (John 8:12)*

He would further speak to me in the years to come through the circumstances of my life, my firefighter's job and His Word, of the lostness of our world and how He wants all to come to Him. I thought of Jim Jones who led 900 to their deaths. I thought of the many Indian gurus that are selling the latest form of light, the many discredited prophets and evangelists that sold people a bill of goods because of marketing. "Just pay this, or channel that, or say something else, or…"

*For such men are false apostles, deceitful workers, disguising themselves as apostles of Christ. And no wonder, for even Satan disguises himself as an **angel of light**. Therefore it is not surprising if his servants also disguise themselves as servants of righteousness. (2 Corinthians 11:13-15)*

The flashlight slips from my hand and
I grope forcefully to regain control
of this silly stick of luminescence.

You Found Me Dave, Come and Taste!

1974, Station One, Alameda Fire Department, 1:30 a.m.

Engine One is first on the scene at another three-story Victorian fire. Smoke and flames are coming from the eaves, front door, and windows. Captain Steckler says, "We're pulling the live line and going in the front door."

Our usual first-in tactic was to enter and find the fire before pouring water on everything. Nozzle in hand, moving low through the darkness, pushing furniture out of the way, I feel the heat increasing and what looks like a vertical sliver of reddish orange light squeezing between the crack of the bedroom door. We find the fire. I push open the door to reveal the inferno dancing before me. I'm strangely drawn as a moth to a flame.

The light seems to be saying, "You found me, Dave! Come and taste!" I can see everything in the room clearly, but this time the light is a counterfeit. It is destroying as it consumes everything in its path. And no wonder, for even Satan disguises himself as an angel of light. As I open the nozzle and hit the fire with a 60 degree fog pattern, it retreats to blackness. Hot, wet smoke and heat blow by me like a snarling cat lashing out at our assault.

Be of sober spirit, and be on the alert. Your adversary, the devil, prowls about like a roaring lion, seeking whom he may devour. *(1 Peter 5:8-9)*

I dropped to the floor for cooler temperatures. Captain Steckler reaches for the nozzle and says, "Search the back of the house; I'll take over."

Search the house? I can't even see the house! I could hear Engine Three and Truck One arriving. *Yeah! Reinforcements are here.* We always need more help because of cuts in manpower. Voices are now apparent in the smoke. I hear crashing glass and furniture, the forceful sounds of axes and saws in operation throughout the structure. I crawl toward what I think is the rear of the house feeling for anything that seemed familiar, a chair, a bed, a table, a rug, or the thing that worries me the most, a body. Pulling the Maglight from my pocket, I turn it on and notice that I can see the beam of light reminiscent of a Star Wars light saber stretched out maybe two feet ahead of me. The sound of my breathing in the air mask is strangely like the breathing of Darth Vader. The tank of air on my back is rated for one-half hour but I usually suck it down in twenty minutes or less. The density of the smoke mixed with steam and darkness was just too much for the light to overcome. I wish I could better explain the feeling. It's as if I'm following this three-inch beam of light, and the only time I see anything is when the light actually touches it. I have the overpowering sense that I'm

205

following this beam and not controlling it.

The flashlight slips from my hand and I grope forcefully to regain control of this silly stick of luminescence. Without it I would be truly lost. I turn a corner and come face to face with the yellow glowing eyes of a terrified cat. She screams and I scream back. My heart skips about five beats and for a moment I want to bolt for the door, but then I realize I can't even find the door. In what seems like hours, but in fact may be only four minutes, the truckies have opened the roof, which releases trapped smoke. As fresh air rushes

in, I can see again. Relief comes as I find that I'm in the middle of the kitchen and have a safe exit with no people needing rescue. *Ah! Liberation.* Again I am reminded of God's Word to me that you will never be lost if you hold onto the Light (Holy Spirit). "Lamp" is used in the sense of a guide in **Psalm 119:105**; and it, of course, often signifies the Lord, or The Light Himself.

1978 - Nine Years a Firefighter, One Year a Christian

I had a great desire to know God, and show Him to all who would listen. It was at a time in my life when I had very few answers to this longing but I was hungry to learn of my Creator. Looking through the mirror of time back some 27 years, I have become aware that the Holy Spirit had always been there in my life, first wooing me through the heritage of a godly pioneering minister grandfather, and a mother widowed before her time. The loss of my father, a circumstance beyond my control; and then, while on vacation, being at the mercy of the Pacific Ocean ten miles off the coast of San Simeon in my father-in-law's boat which was on fire, brought me to the realization that I, again, could not control my own situation and may, in fact, die. Four years later sitting in a Methodist church that seemingly didn't know of the Holy Spirit but for some reason in the memory banks of some church elders, they felt the church should have a revival. The revival team that showed up (Foursquare Gospel) was not of our denomination, and seemed strange. They asked us to bring Bibles, to pray, hold hands, and sing some new songs. Sunday morning most of the church went forward to receive Christ. I don't know about anyone else that day but the Holy Spirit showed up for me and shined His light on Jesus, who became my Savior and Lord.

Light and darkness have been apparent to me since my camping experience. Many times alone in the darkness of a building fire waiting for ventilation or portable light to be brought in from a second and third arriving apparatus, I would grope through the blackness hoping that soon the lights would be turned on. The light could do two things, one to illuminate, the other to blind. If we weren't careful, we could be blinded by the light directed into our eyes instead of ahead of us. From pitch black to bright light in the eyes, it's hard to tell which is worse. God has also taught me a lesson from those experiences. The work of the Holy Spirit is not for Himself. We may sum up the teachings regarding the Spirit in these following statements: He is the Spirit of truth; He guides into all truth; He brings to memory Christ's teachings; He shows things to come; He glorifies Christ; He speaks not of Himself but of Christ; He, like believers, bears witness to Christ; He enables

I Could Have Died A Thousand Deaths

Christians to do the works of Christ, but always in sync with the Bible. He convicts the world of sin, righteousness, and judgment; He came because Christ ascended.

He is another Comforter; one who comes alongside. He is to abide with believers forever. In other words, the Holy Spirit helps us to see Jesus clearly; He directs our path to God. Paul, on the Damascus Road, thought he was right in seeking out and killing Christians until Jesus, with the help of the Holy Spirit, brought light to Paul's understanding of the Scriptures.

Now Saul, still breathing threats and murder against the disciples of the Lord, went to the high priest, and asked for letters from him to the synagogues at Damascus, so that if he found any belonging to the Way [believers], *both men and women, he might bring them bound to Jerusalem. And it came about that as he journeyed, he was approaching Damascus, and suddenly a* <u>*light from heaven*</u> *flashed around him.* **(Acts 9:1-3)**

With the best of intentions we can easily get off track unless we daily continue in His Word with the help of the Holy Spirit. Some of the movements in Christianity today have been confused. So many people are running to the latest happening of the Spirit. Let's giggle, let's dance, let us… we want… fill me… They run looking <u>into</u> a light and are blinded by it. If they would turn 180 degrees and see where the light is shining (on Jesus), they would be blessed and able to help others. In the following verses, Paul is in prison and will soon be executed. He is turning over his work to Timothy, his disciple, and warning him:

I solemnly charge you in the presence of God and of Christ Jesus, who is to judge the living and the dead, and by His appearing and His kingdom: preach the word **[Light]***; be ready in season and out of season; reprove, rebuke, exhort, with great patience and* *instruction. For the time will come when they will not endure* **sound [teaching]** *but wanting to have their ears tickled, they will accumulate for themselves teachers in accordance to their own desires; and will turn away their ears from the* **truth**, *and will turn aside to* **myths**. *But you, be sober in all things, endure hardship, do the work of an evangelist, fulfill your ministry.* **(2 Timothy 4:1-5)**

The insistence on faithfulness and sound teaching is the more necessary because of the danger of apostasy in the churches. **Ears tickled:** People will wish to hear what satisfies their sinful desires. Paul is writing about the church but it is also a picture of our world, which desperately needs the true Light, **Jesus Christ.**

"Stand at the cross✝roads and look;
Ask for the ancient path [His story],
Ask where the good way is, walk in it,
And you will find rest for your souls."
(Jeremiah 6:16)

This is My Story

This is my story, this is my song,
Life's been so lovely living so long.
The names are the same, no aliases used,
All stories are true, no fiction abused.
I thank you for reading my ramblings and clues,
For a life lived so well, but not nearly so smooth!

EPILOGUE

A Final Word

A final word to you, my friend. If you have arrived at this point, you have perseverance. You have what it takes to think about your mortality. There comes a day when all of us will stand before a righteous God. Will you be ready? I am, and I would love to see you there on that joyous day. It doesn't take work on your part, just a response to God. All the days of church going and the practice of being a "good person" is not enough unless you take the time to check out the Book to see if you are on the right track. Could you be just spinning your wheels? How would you know unless you have checked out God's manual? There are four verses that I think sum it all up:

(Romans 10:9-11)

*That if you **confess** with your mouth the Lord Jesus and **believe** in your heart that God has raised Him from the dead, you will be saved. For with the **heart** one believes unto righteousness, and with the **mouth** confession is made unto **salvation**. For the Scripture says, "Whoever believes on Him will not be put to shame."*

And Jesus says, *(John 3:16, 17)*

*For God so loved the world that **He gave** His only begotten Son, that **whoever believes** in Him should not perish but have everlasting life. For God did not send His Son into the world to condemn the world, but that the world through Him might be saved.*

Please don't let pride get in the way. We have all done things we shouldn't have. Let Jesus fix those; He has a gift for all of us. A gift is given, but the recipient must receive that gift or it goes unopened. Please, my friend, open your gift, which is the "peace that passes all understanding to guard your heart and mind in Christ Jesus," and join me.

If you would like to discuss this further, please contact me at lemoine@charter.net

Dave LeMoine

Made in the USA
San Bernardino, CA
10 January 2016